500 Tidbits of Insight

Living with and Overcoming Depression

ISBN: 0692202587
ISBN 13: 9780692202586

*For all those that walk in the darkness searching
for any kind of light.*

Preface

When I was seventeen, I was diagnosed with depression. This diagnosis was later modified to include colorful adjectives like 'severe', 'major', and 'with suicidal tendencies'. What followed was nothing short of a nightmare. I tried my best to be fully compliant with a treatment plan I only sometimes understood, which was created by a team of people who deeply loved me and cared for me. I followed advice, even when it felt more like following orders. I fought for my life at a time when most people around me failed to comprehend that 'depression' was not a mood I could remove from my body by snapping my fingers, but rather was a bizarre shadow that tried constantly to suffocate me to death.

I desperately needed something to help me deal with my new life filled with bossy, opinionated people. I hoped that someone had walked in these depression shoes before me and left behind some kind of book to reach for during long nights and troubling days, a book I could read despite side effects of medication, progressing symptoms, and my sadly diminishing optimism. I looked and found memoirs, some of which are very well written. However, I found it hard to relate to complete strangers. I turned to self-help books written by some of the best medical professionals. However, they too fell short. They often promoted a particular style of working through specific aspects of the condition or explained new ideas in such depth that it would have been difficult to benefit much from them without working with someone in person. It was out of the frustration of not finding a book written in a style that I desired when I needed it most that the idea for this book originated. This book's existence is meant to fill that void I discovered while undergoing treatment. What I desperately needed was something more than a memoir or a systematic and complicated self-help book. I needed something to reach for during all the in-between times. The times I spent in-between appointments, in-between states of pain, in-between states of various methods of waiting.

This book is what I wanted to reach for. It is a collection of all the things I learned and realistic applications of all the advice I received. When writing it, I referenced my journals, notebooks, and my limited, yet strangely comforting memories. Since its contents stem from decades of living, I cannot pinpoint with any accuracy where these ideas originally crossed my path. If anything seems familiar, it probably is either a true word of wisdom or just a pleasant coincidence.

I tried to make this book as useful as possible. I wrote it to be read any way you like. You can read it from start to finish, you can open to a random page, or you can skim it. You can reread it several times. You can read it for ideas to discuss at your next appointment with your medical professional. You can reference it to brainstorm methods of explaining what you are going through when you next talk to your family and loved ones. It can be read by someone just learning about depression, someone in the middle of another year of the medical condition, or by a family member of someone who suffers from it.

The book is meant to be a companion during your journey of discovery about mental illness, its treatment, the recovery from it, and how it changes anyone that is even remotely in its path. It is not a replacement for appropriate medical help from licensed professionals. It is not a substitute for real people that you interact with, have relationships with, or desire to know better.

I recommend keeping this book somewhere useful where you can get to it when you need a bit of goodness and hope. Keep it by your bedside, in your purse, in your car, or hide it under your sofa. Do whatever works for you. Just know you are not alone. These words are here to ease your burden, even if for just a few minutes of time. Together, this collection can help you hold on during the in-between times. A gift, I assure you, my younger self would have loved to have received.

I truly wish you the best on this road you are traveling,

-K.

1. The situation you are in is temporary. You may feel a desire to panic. Try to not let this happen. The pain and suffering you are currently feeling will go away. It might take time, but it will pass. There is a day in your future when you will not be in this pain. There is a day in your future when you will not be suffering in this way anymore.

2. Give your body permission to be sad sometimes. The human body is not designed to be happy all of the time. There are going to be times when you feel horrible. Having a day filled with negative moods might not mean that your depression is getting worse. It may mean you are just having natural negative emotions to events in your life that are worthy of acknowledgement by way of sadness or disappointment. Give yourself permission to be upset about things that you need to be upset about.

3. Making a list of goals is good, but reinventing the way you define accomplishment is better. It is okay and probably necessary to give yourself credit for actions and tasks that were second-nature before developing depression. Create or buy a bigger planner that has the room for you to list things like getting out of bed, eating breakfast, and changing your socks. Enjoy the satisfaction of crossing off every item on your list. The everyday stuff is hard work and you deserve to give yourself credit for doing it well.

4. There will be a delay between making the changes you need to get better and actually feeling better. If you know that you are doing what you need to do, give yourself a break. Your body might just need some time to heal itself and positively react to the wonderful work you are doing to get better. Continue to comply with the treatment, keep your doctor appointments, and stay consistent. Maintaining a routine and schedule most certainly will help you heal more quickly.

5. It is always okay to ask for help. You may have to ask several different people before you get the help you are looking for, but keep asking. Not everyone can provide you with the kind of help you are looking for, so do not feel bad if you have to keep searching for assistance. You may even need to ask the same person more than once and that too is okay.

6. Having some kind of a hobby is good. At its severest, depression may make it difficult to take up a hobby, but once you have the energy, try to make it a priority. You may not feel joy from the activity the first time you try it, but keep at it. Give it a real chance to become your new favorite pastime. Also continue to pursue activities that you used to enjoy doing. You deserve to have comforting and, if possible, enjoyable fun habits in your schedule.

7. Get in the habit of saying thank you. It may take a long time and lots of work to get the help you need. By the time you receive it, you may seem exhausted and bitter because it took so long to get something you desperately needed, but tell the person you are thankful for their help anyway. It is the first step towards forming a positive relationship with the person and encourages him or her to take the time to help you in the future. It is the simplest, easiest way to acknowledge that something positive has happened to you. It may be a small act, but it solidifies your commitment to getting better.

8. Instead of asking what is normal, begin to ask what is normal *for you*. A popular movie or song may spark a type of emotional reaction in the people around you, but not you. This is okay. Part of the healing process is the acceptance your unique self. Try your best to not obsess about recovery or proceed through the treatment at a speed similar to other people. Whatever you are feeling is exactly how you should be feeling. However long it takes to begin to feel okay again is exactly how long you need.

9. Developing depression was not your fault. This is not a reflection of you or your actions. You did nothing wrong. Humanness comes with unpredictable experiences, but their happening does not make you somehow a lesser being. Living and coping with depression is hard. Choosing to believe that you are still a person of great value does not have to be. As with anyone dealing with an illness, your actions today may be limited, but that does not mean that your actions are not notable.

10. You can always control your attitude. Even if today you were perfectly healthy, you would not be able to control everything. When living with depression, it can easily seem like nothing is within your control, but that would be a false statement. You can always choose how you are going to evaluate anything you observe or experience. Not all emotions or thoughts are within your control, but the opinions you have often are. You can choose to hope for a positive experience while waiting for the bus, for food to finish cooking, or to speak to someone. You can choose to be thankful for what you own. No one and no illness can take this choice from you.

11. Practice will pay off. Just as an athlete or a musician must practice daily in order to improve at their craft, you will now need to practice new life skills daily. It is not beneath you or a sign of failure to make it priority to practice new habits. By taking the time to form new, healthier habits, you can begin to create a healthier life. Coping with and recovering from depression is going to take some work. It is by practicing a consistent, steady routine of healthier behavior and thoughts that you probably will, in time, start to feel better.

12. Not all depressions are the same. If you experience more than one episode of depression, you may need a slightly different treatment plan for each episode. It is normal to make modifications to your health care. You may even need to try a different medication or a different kind of therapy. Sometimes the same regiment works, and sometimes not. Don't worry if you need to attempt new things. Give yourself permission to accept the current situation and react to it the way you need to.

13. Different people experience depression differently. While there are people that experience an episode of depression and work through it to live out the rest of their life depression free, there are those that experience depression as a true chronic illness. It may be unhelpful to assume that one person's experience with depression is the exact same as another's. Be open to accepting how your unique body is developing clinical depression.

14. There are no shortcuts. Recovery will most likely follow effort and work done by you. You are most likely going to need to comply with some kind of treatment plan over a length of time in order to get well. The severe medical condition you are experiencing will not simply vanish if you ignore it long enough. You might be able to temporary ignore mild symptoms for a very short while, but clinical depression when left untreated often increases in its severity. Seeking out professional medical help early is a good idea.

15. It is not a competition. You may encounter people who have an expectation that you will get well in some time frame they have invented in their minds. Ignore all of that. You are not racing against someone else's clock to get well. You have not done anything wrong if you are not well by this invented and often arbitrary timeline of progress. Take the time you need and stop competing with others.

16. Exercise is great, but not the answer to every problem. Physical movement of your body will probably help you feel better. The important thing to focus on is simply movement. Give yourself credit for walking and standing. Try not to stress over completing traditional exercises. Focus on what you are comfortable doing. If you only have the energy to walk for a few minutes, then fine. Do what you can, move when you can, and give yourself a break. As long as you are trying your best, pushing yourself a little every day, then you are doing fine.

17. Accept feedback, but don't take it personally. This is easier said than done, but you need to try your best to listen to feedback.

There are going to be times when your ability to accurately sense the world around you is a bit off. The feedback that people give you may be useful, but only to a degree. Unfortunately, it does not take much for the feedback you receive to take on a life of its own and begin to become a put down. Sometimes the feedback can be extremely hurtful, if you let it. Focus on the useful bits and mentally trash the rest. Someone telling you that you are taking forever to make a decision is only useful in that you now know your sense of time is a bit off. You can disregard the implication that you are purposely wasting time, that you are defective, or otherwise doing anything wrong. You are not. The person communicating to you may just lack tact. That is a reflection of their communication skills, not your self-worth.

18. Depression is more than a mood disorder. It is a common misconception that if you are depressed, you are just sad all the time. There is a lot more to depression than this. Your physical body most likely hurts a lot. Traditional pain medicines and remedies might not be helping. Simple tasks may now feel impossible because they are painful. Clinical depression has many symptoms, make sure to acknowledge all aspects of the medical condition.

19. Simplify your wardrobe. Focus on being responsible for a week or two weeks' worth of clothes at most. You are dealing with a severe illness. It is okay if you wear the same shoes every day for a while. It is okay if you forgo makeup or simplify what you take the time to do. Just focus on bathing regularly, wearing clean clothes, and otherwise basic maintenance. There is no need to impress anyone right now. Just focus on being healthy.

20. You might not like every doctor or therapist you meet. You want to work with doctors and therapists that you respect and trust. It is less important that you like them. At times, you probably will not. If they are doing their job well, he or she will have to tell you things that are difficult for you to hear and understand. It will probably frustrate you and you may not like your doctor for a while. It is okay to feel this way, just continue with your commitment to seeking care.

21. You are not the only one. Depression is not new. You are not the first person to develop this mental illness. There are those who did not overcome it and there are many who have. This means that there are many people you can turn to throughout your healing process. If your family and friends are unable to help you, you have people you can turn to. There are many support groups, many stories of this type of journey, and many opportunities to connect with others so you never have to be alone in your recovery.

22. Don't obsessively worry about how your pain affects others. The adults in your life are responsible for their health, not you. If people you know seem to pull away, let them. They may need a little bit more space to recharge and process how best to help you. Some may pull away completely. Let them. What you are experiencing is difficult for those who love you to watch, and some may be too weak to stay by your side. Forgive them and let them go. Allow room for others to enter into your life.

23. Sometimes your feelings or moods don't make sense. That happens. It is part of experiencing a mental illness. It is typical and common. Some days are going to be better than others, which in a way makes your feelings even stranger. Remind yourself that you are not going crazy. This is just the clinical depression. It will get better and the unpredictable moods are temporary and will, in time, stabilize.

24. Depression is a big deal. It might change you a lot. Be prepared to come out of it with different interests and opinions. It is okay if you don't like a sports team or movie anymore and your new favorite snack has changed. Don't attempt to return to who you were before the illness. Instead, move forward towards a reinvented, stronger version of you.

25. You will probably receive some bad advice. Not everyone will or can be supportive. Sometimes a person will attempt to offer advice or help that frankly is more hurtful than helpful. You are going through something that most cannot imagine. It is to be expected that sometimes their best intentions fall short. Do not expect every piece of advice you hear to be good for you.

26. The stigma may seem bad, but that is not your problem to fix. Do not waste your energy talking about your experiences with depression with literally everyone. Form a supportive network of people and focus on just you. Today, direct your strength on getting better. If later on in life, you wish to be an advocate for others, you can, but not now. Now, you need to be you and that you is not well and needs your full attention to get better.

27. Do not expect anyone or anything to swoop in and cure you. There is no magic pill that you take just once and instantly you feel better. There is no specialist that is so talented that after one visit with him or her, you will feel well. It took time for clinical depression to develop and it will take time for your body to recover. Try your best to be patient.

28. The treatment sucks, do it anyway. Hopefully, at some point in the future there will be an easy way to diagnose and treat clinical depression. However, today is not that day. The best method of treatment is not efficient and painless. It takes time to work and it does not work for everyone on the first attempt. Despite all of this, you should comply with a treatment plan made with the guidance of medical professionals. That plan of action is the best one available right now and you deserve the very best.

29. You may never know what caused your depression or why it happened. Sometimes, depression appears to be the body reacting to a big life event, but this is not always the case. Many suffer from depression and a cause is never discovered. Do your best to not obsess about finding a logical cause and instead focus on moving towards a healthier future.

30. Your mind is probably not working efficiently right now. Part of what is making you ill is that your mind is not thinking in a way that is healthy. It is processing ideas and information in a manner that is disrupting your ability to function well. Your beliefs and opinions are valid and real. What needs to change is the way you use your beliefs and opinions to make decisions. You also need to be open to expanding those beliefs and opinions to account for new experiences including developing depression. It may take a long time to adapt, but in time it will get easier.

31. Write down your concerns to share with your medical professional. Identify the most important and most urgent on your list. Your memory, if it has not already, is likely going to become unreliable. You likely will forget to report a symptom or unusual mood experience if you do not note when these things happen between appointments. By coming prepared, you can improve the quality of your care. Just keep in mind that you might not be able to discuss everything in one appointment so make sure to prioritize your list. If you do not get to an item, bring it up next time.

32. You might end up in a hospital, and that is okay. When people get really sick, they may end up in the hospital. If clinical depression makes you severely sick, you may spend some time as a patient in one. This is not a sign that you are incurable or somehow permanently defective. It is an indication that your body needs the extra support and care, so allow medical professionals at the hospital to do their best to take care of you. Listen to their suggestions and follow up with your regular health care providers.

33. Modify your social commitments. Now is not the time to attempt to plan social gatherings or big events. You need to be selective about when you hang out with people. Try to attend group events that allow you to share the responsibility, but not become overwhelmed by it. If you are usually someone who spends a lot of time alone at home, schedule outings so that you are around people. It is important to leave your house and simply be around people. Even a small commitment, like spending an hour each week walking in a nearby park, downtown, or local mall, will likely help.

34. The road to recovery is not straight and steep. When you start to get better, it likely is not going to be steady and constant. You may perhaps still have bad moments when you are very symptomatic while overall, you are getting much better. Accept that these are just minor events and try not to give them too much attention. If you overreact, you can make the symptoms last longer. Acknowledge that you are having some symptoms, make adjustments, but continue to move forward.

35. You can do something about your situation. No matter where you are or how you feel, there is always something you can do. Occasionally the best action is to leave the room or just look away. You might try focusing on your breathing or thinking about something different for a few moments. It is okay to feel overwhelmed sometimes. It happens to everyone.

36. Trying to reconnect with the people you care about most can be difficult. Having a simple conversation may seem impossible. One way to contribute is to share observations. The weather is a popular topic, but you can try looking around you. Maybe you will discover something uncommon. Share that discovery with the people you are with. It might be a great conversation starter. Occasionally what you say might not spark further conversation and that's okay. Keep trying because in time it will get easier to converse with others.

37. Make a routine to calm down. Extreme moods, extreme pain, or a mixture of both might make your suffering hard to deal with, so having a plan of action in place is helpful. Select activities you can do to calm yourself and to provide some relief. It might take some trial and error, but establishing a plan of action for these situations is one way to relieve stress and anxiety.

38. There are going to be times when it is the depression talking. You may feel or say something that is not true or goes against your thoughts or beliefs. It may even really hurt someone you care about. While you might not have control over what your body is feeling, you are still responsible for it. It is unfair that you may have to apologize or deal with the consequences of actions that you did not want to commit, but you probably will have to. Attempt to not to let the actions of the clinical depression become your personality. You are you and the illness is the illness.

39. Make the best decision you can with the information you have. You might not have all the information you want before you need to make a decision. Just focus on doing your best today, it is okay if your choice is not fantastic. Occasionally, a fantastic option is not available and the best choice is simply less bad than alternatives. It happens, you have not failed at anything, just make the most of your situation.

40. Consider meeting with a diet coach or nutritionist. Clinical depression is a severe medical condition with multiple symptoms. Among your symptoms, you may be having issues with your diet or eating. Consulting a specialist may benefit you while you are coping with your illness. He or she might be able to provide new ideas or strategies for eating healthy while you are recovering.

41. When making a decision regarding a major life change, ask if it is the best fit for you. It is easy to get caught up in the idea that if something is good for others, then it must be good for you too. That might not be true. The best ranked school you get admitted to might have a learning environment which leaves you feeling uncomfortable. You might receive a job offer from a well-respected company, but the schedule would negatively impact your ability to continue with your health care. When making the tough decisions, think about what you need, not what looks good on paper. Select what is best for you and your life.

42. We are all connected and impact each other. Often we do not realize this or even understand how exactly we do so. When you are having a good day and smile at strangers, it impacts them. If you are having a bad day, and take it out on others, this also impacts them. While it is not your responsibility to make everyone around you feel good, it is your responsibility to treat others with respect. If you are experiencing a negative mood, then now might not be the time to run errands. Wait an hour, have a snack, or go for a walk first. Acknowledge that you share this world with others and attempt to make positive connections.

43. It is not your place to judge others. You may know that someone could do more. You may disagree with a decision they have made. It is not your job to pass judgment on them. Just as you have the right to decide how you spend your time, others do too. You may passionately disagree with someone's decision, but it is possible to respect their decision without passing judgment.

44. It is okay to not have all the answers. It is unrealistic to have an expectation that you will always know how to alleviate your symptoms. Even if you had never developed depression, as a human, you are going to have times in your life when you just simply do not know something. That is why it is important to make it a priority to form some kind of healthy support network. It is okay if in the beginning it is made up of only paid medical professionals. The important thing is to have people you trust in your life to ask for advice in finding answers and solutions.

45. Sometimes it will not work. You may follow the advice of a medical professional exactly, and it still does not work. That is okay. It is also okay to get frustrated. Learning how to cope with and work through clinical depression is not an easy process. You are probably going to attempt things that work well for others, but not you. Keep trying because there are many ways to combat the various symptoms of the illness. Through trial and error you will find what works best for you.

46. Keep doing what works even after you feel better. Many people go back to old habits or discontinue taking medication the moment they feel better. This is not a good idea. It was only because of the changes you have made that your body was starting to recover. Even after you have recovered, you are likely at risk for relapse for a period of time afterward. Keep going to your appointments. Depending on how long and severe your depression was, it may be months before it is safe to discontinue the treatment.

47. You have the right to decide what is meaningful to you. It is a big responsibility, but it is you who will choose the story of your life. You can choose how you are going to react and respond to the events of your life. It is your decision if you want to hold grudges or forgive. It is your choice if you wish to be angry or let it go. If you are dissatisfied with how an important event sits with you, then choose to make it less important. If something that others say is not a big deal, really is a big deal to you. Then it is okay to admit that.

48. Depression changing you is not a sign of defeat. You are experiencing a very serious medical condition. It is common and normal for the experience to change you in some way. Most people find they are a much stronger person for having lived through an episode of clinical depression. There is no right or wrong way to be effected by it. You may be a very different person, or you may not be. Accepting that there is no correct way to be altered by the experience is the healthiest thing you can do for yourself.

49. Strive to be an active participant. You need to actively take part in your care and treatment plan. However, doing more may not mean you will heal more quickly. There is no standard formula for seeing results at the rate you wish to see them. Just focus on doing what you can when you can. The more involved you are, the more you may feel hope and optimism.

50. What you are experiencing is real. The human body is not an accurate recording device. Our memories are not extremely accurate down to the last detail. When depressed, it is often even less so. However, this does not mean that what you are experiencing is somehow not a part of reality. It just means that you may perceive or react to your surroundings differently than before. It probably is also different than how other people react to it. What you are experiencing is still part of reality and your reaction is very real.

51. Practice eliminating the 'all or nothing' style of thinking. Many people suffering from clinical depression also suffer from a habitual inner voice that classifies everything as an extreme. If you miss a bus, that inner voice might tell you that you always miss the bus. If you forget to pick up milk that voice might say you never remember to pick up milk. Try to think of one example when you did not miss the bus or one trip to the store when you did pick up milk. Acknowledging counterexamples to this negative voice is something you can do on your own to help overcome this unhealthy habit.

52. Create a dream board or collage. It can be difficult to understand how making small changes today can impact your future and make it better. Imagining what kind of future you want is a good exercise. Sometimes making an actual physical dream board, or notebook, filled with drawings, pictures, and short descriptions of the future you want is helpful. When you can visualize the future you want to build for yourself, it will likely be easier to make decisions today that take you towards that goal.

53. Focus your time on a few projects. It is easy to take on a lot of different projects and attempt to work towards many goals at once, but do not do that. Instead, redirect your time and energy to tackling one thing at a time. There may be many things you want to try to help your depression, but master one before moving onto another. During your recovery, it will be hard to work on several personal projects at once. It is better to complete one task than to have several dozen in progress. This simplification might relieve a lot of stress.

54. Research and learn about clinical depression. While every person is unique and depression affects everyone differently, learning about how others have dealt with depression is very beneficial. This information can help you form realistic goals about your own recovery and treatment process. It may also provide some hope to learn that others have struggled with and overcome experiences similar to your own.

55. Write your own story. For every account you will hear about a survivor of clinical depression, it may seem like there are a dozen that continue to live with it every day. It can be helpful to hear how others have lived with or coped with depression, but at the end of the day, your life is truly yours. The way you handle the depression is also yours. You decide how much time and energy you devote to your recovery. That is your choice and your story to write. No one else can write it for you.

56. Others may not seek treatment. That is not your burden to carry. Throughout the process of receiving treatment for depression, you may realize that there are people in your life with unhealthy habits or who perhaps also suffer from a form of mental illness. You cannot make another person seek help or expect them be receptive to confrontations to change. If the relationship you have with someone is unhealthy or negatively impacting your ability to recover from your mental illness, you may need to let go of that relationship. You may need to open your heart and mind to letting other, healthier people into your life.

57. You don't have to finish every little thing that you start. Every so often you attempt something and midway through start to realize that it will bring you no joy or benefit to complete the project. Finishing might also not bring you any sense of accomplishment. It is okay to let it go. Just make sure you actually and fully discontinue the project. You deserve peace of mind. Admitting midway through projects that your priorities have changed is not an act of failure, but an act of progress. Sometimes only by doing can you learn what you value most. Sometimes letting go is a sign of achievement in itself.

58. The universe is not in debt to you. At some point during the healing process, you may feel that someone, or even the world, owes you something. You may aim to justify that all the pain you are experiencing is some kind of a price to pay. It is not. Clinical depression is horrible. It is painful and it is simply just awful. What exactly you gain from the experience is what you choose to gain from it.

59. Consider living life by the minute or hour. A day may be too much time to think about, so do not think of time in this manner. Instead, just focus on the immediate future. Identify what you need or want to do in the next hour. Try not to think about something happening next week or revisit an event that occurred yesterday. Instead, focus on what you are working on right now, this minute. It will take some practice, but once you master this then your clinical depression may seem a lot more manageable.

60. Simplify your cooking. While you are dealing with the serious illness that is clinical depression, you need to make foods that are simple. There is no need to burden your time with recipes that have several steps and require lots of ingredients. Keep it simple. Look for ways to make eating less stressful. When you do cook, make a few servings so you can have leftovers to quickly reheat later. Make an attempt to create meals that require no cooking at all.

61. Making decisions is stressful. Even decisions that you used to make without thinking can seem like a huge obstacle. Clinical depression is possibly causing this. For a while, the smallest choices you want to make may seem impossible. It is okay to feel a little overwhelmed by this stress. Right now, it is most likely a victory every time you pick something to eat or wear. It is okay to allow these decisions to be noteworthy accomplishments because right now, they are.

62. Take a break from social media. While battling depression, interpersonal relationships that you handle in person will possibly be very challenging. Online commitments, even small ones, will add stress to your life, which you do not need right now. Limit your interactions on the internet. Stick to reading and gathering information, but limiting how often you take the time to respond or comment. This simple change might relieve a lot of your stress.

63. Gather information about your thoughts. Attempt to write down what you are thinking exactly. For most coping with a form of depression, an inner dialogue is forming in your head that may be extremely negative. If you are able to record parts of this dialogue it might help your treatment. It can provide insight into your thoughts and sharing these notes with a medical professional will aid in their ability to assist in your recovery.

64. Take a minute vacation. You don't have to leave the house to have a break and relax. Take one minute and for that time think about something new and different, something that you do not have a strong emotional reaction to. This way, you can give your intense emotions a break, even if for just a minute. With practice, you can extend your breaks to several minutes or an hour, but start very small. If you are having a rough day, take a fifteen second vacation. All aspects of you need a break from time to time, including your emotions, so give them one.

65. You do not owe anyone an explanation. You really do not. You probably do not have the energy to respond to every request for an explanation. If you do respond to someone's request, make it simple. You are allowed to tell someone that you are busy, that you are unavailable, or that you have other commitments. You do not have to explain what you are busy doing, why you are unavailable, or what kind of other commitments you have. Frankly, that is not the business of others. If someone that insists on knowing, he or she might not be looking out for your best interests. You are allowed to have a private life.

66. Accurately record your emotions. The concept of a mood diary is an old one and one that many try. It can be helpful to ask yourself how you feel right now and then record that information. It may be helpful to do this frequently in order to discover if there are any patterns to your moods or emotions. There may be and this type of information gathering could provide the insight you need to relieve a lot of stress and pain. However, if you do this, share this information with your doctor so that he or she can also use the information to help you too.

67. Go outside. You do not need to have a destination in mind, just go. It does not need to be for long, even if you stand outside for a few minutes, this is good. Reconnecting with the outside world, even for just a few moments, is probably good for you. It can go a long way to reconnecting you to the world in a positive way. Try finding words to describe the noises you hear. Try identifying what you smell and taste. Focus on your senses. This exercise, no matter how brief may be very beneficial.

68. You do not have to explaining everything. When you were diagnosed with a mental illness, you did not also become the voice box for this serious medical condition. It is not your job to discuss, describe, and explain what it is or is not. Your number one job right now is to get well, which will take a lot of your time and energy. Spend your limited energy on you and do not worry about educating other people about the illness. There are many people working on that problem for you so that you do not have to. Right now, just focus on you.

69. Small things might cause big reactions and that is okay. You may have very extreme reactions to tiny things right now. Depression makes it difficult to prioritize what is important to you because everything might seem equally important or equally problematic. It is hard to know what bothers you the most when everything seems to be the problem. It is alright to let a small thing impact you greatly once in a while. Doing so does not mean that your personality has taken a permanent turn into drama land. It just means you need extra emotions right now to deal with something and that is fine.

70. Not every day is going to be a day of progress. There will be horrible, awful days that seem to be the worst things you have experienced ever. Believe it or not, but every individual that has endured a form of depression has experienced these kinds of days. Really, every single person has. The road to recovery will likely have some of these days. You most likely will have moments when it seems like you have made no progress, but you undoubtedly have.

71. Change your environment when you can. Occasionally everything, every little thing may be bothering you. If you can, then remove some of the items that are bothersome. Turn off a bright light, change clothes, go barefoot, or just look in a different direction. A small change can have a profound impact, and there are small changes you can make no matter where you are. It just might take a few moments to realize what they are, and some might be hard to discover, but give it a go. It may provide a small amount of immediate relief.

72. Create a spot for your most important things. Designate a location for your most used and important items like keys, glasses, driver's license, and cell phone. Consider making a bowl or box as your important stuff holder. Get in the habit of putting your small, most used items there and looking there first when you need them. In time, you will not need to remember where you put these items because you are in the habit of putting them in the same spot every time.

73. Invest the time to make an advanced appointment book. Imagine a traditional appointment book, but with more pieces of information about your daily life, including scheduled times to eat and sleep. That is most likely what you need. Some are comfortable with making one on their smart phone or computer. Others need to hold it in their hands and may benefit best from a traditional planner. Write down every appointment and important event that requires your presence. Consider including everything from social commitments and bathroom breaks to reminders to bathe. Work on developing the habit to check it often, even every hour. This probably will help you take care of yourself by decreasing the stress and anxiety of remembering all this stuff inside your head.

74. Make procedural checklists. Before taking the brave steps towards bigger projects, make a checklist. Break down tasks into smaller, easy to accomplish parts. Part of coping with your depression may even involve leaving reminder checklists at key locations. Your bedtime routine might need to be written down as a checklist and taped to your bathroom mirror. You may find yourself needing a checklist to make a cup of coffee. This is all okay. You are not going crazy if you do anything like this. You are being responsible.

75. You do not have to do everything that people advise you to do. Every so often the advice you get is horrible. People may feel that since they know what to do to feel better, then they are now the expert on what makes everyone happy. Their logic is that since you both are human, then as a fellow human it must work for you too. It is faulty logic. Generally people mean well, but their idea is not practical. It is okay if this irritates you.

76. You have time. Your life path can and will wait while you help yourself. The reality is that you are dealing with a severe medical condition. This is a big deal and deserves to be respected as such. You are likely still able to do all of your big life plans and dreams, you will have the time, but right now, today, focus just on you. Focus on working towards a healthier future.

77. Take a new route. Leave several minutes earlier than usual and take a different route to your destination. Travel down a different street, or consider traveling by different means. You could even travel by one mode half way there and then walk the rest of the way. This small new experience may help several of your symptoms including your memory. Small new experiences may, over time, help redevelop your memory skills.

78. Attempt to reduce the stress in your life. It is easier said than done, but you might ponder that there are different ways you may be under stress. If you are unable to relieve your emotional stress right now then attempt relieving some physical stress. Try stretching or a warm bath. Calming music is helpful for some, but it most certainly will take some trial and error to discover what kinds of actions reduce stress for you. Once something works, it may not work every single time, but continue trying new ways of relaxing.

79. Prioritize which activities you are going to do first. It will be easier to focus and, over time, you will improve your attention span if you do only one thing at a time. Try to avoid distractions and interruptions. Consider turning off electronics when you sit down to read, do a craft, or do other hands on activities. When you are on a computer, try to finish reading or exploring one website before opening up another. It may also reduce your stress level to worry about and focus on one thing at a time.

80. Make mental connections. When you hear an idea you like, or learn something you want to remember, attempt to make a connection between the new information and your existing knowledge. It is a well-known trick to help your mind practice forming associations. Making these kinds of mental connections may help your ability to concentrate and remember information. Often, depression negatively impacts these abilities, but through practice you might regain these skills. It takes time and patience. It is okay if you get frustrated, just keep trying.

81. Leave positive notes for yourself. Create notes with uplifting messages, even really cheesy ones, and then place them so you will rediscover them later. Tape a note of encouragement on your alarm clock so it is the first thing you see in the morning. Tape a positive note on your toothpaste, so it is one of the last things you see before you go to bed. They can be quotes from people you admire or simple phrases of goodness. You might not believe in them in the beginning of this exercise, but just seeing positive words over time might help lift your spirits.

82. Give yourself a time buffer. Leave for appointments, school, work, and other meetings a few minutes earlier than usual. That way if something out of your control happens, you probably will make it to the commitment on time. Showing up to important events on schedule will decrease your stress level and this habit might help you stay organized.

83. Pick your battles. You cannot fight every single argument or battle you are invited to participate in, so do not try to. Be selective about which one you are going to devote your energy to right now. Put all others off until a later time or choose to not participate in them at all. You have the right to choose which battles you want to fight.

84. You do not have to have an opinion. You may spend days and weeks learning about something only to be just as indifferent as when you started. That is okay. You do not have to have a strong opinion about everything. It might seem like everyone you know likes or loves something, but you do not. That is fine. It does not mean you do not care, it just means you do not have a favorite or a side you favor. There is nothing wrong with that.

85. You can still contribute. Clinical depression may impact your ability to make the kinds of contributions to your community and to the relationships you have worked to establish. Having any kind of serious medical condition potentially impacts the types of contributions you can make, but not your ability to contribute. You are still able to help out from time to time. You can still make a positive impact. The only really difference is what you can do to have that kind of an impact. It may feel like you are doing less, but keep doing what you can. Offer to help with small things if an overall project seems too big to tackle. There is nothing wrong with doing the small stuff. It needs to get done too.

86. You may not know how you feel sometimes. You may not know what is bothering you today. You may not know what you want to do in the future. That is okay if occasionally you simply just do not know. Give yourself a break and think about or do something else for a while. Forcing the issue may only add stress anyway, so spend some time not worrying about it. Revisit the issue later.

87. Your ability to communicate may be hindered. It is okay. What you think you say and the words that escape from your mouth may be different. Listen to the feedback a person might give you in a conversation. Look at their body language. Focus on figuring out if you are actually communicating what you intend to. If not, back out of the conversation and trying again later. If you cannot, then simply stop talking for a few moments. Take a deep breath, fake a yawn if you have to, and then start again. Everyone misspeaks occasionally.

88. It may be physically painful to think. If you find yourself in a situation where the simple act of concentrating on an idea is painful, you are not imaging this. It is most certainly happening. You did not do anything wrong. The severe medical condition that is clinical depression may cause you to have moments when your head just really hurts. It may even hurt so much that you have some difficulty thinking about simple ideas. It is okay. This will pass.

89. Don't expect others to understand. Instead, seek out people who are kind. Compassion is most likely what you need right now. A person does not need to understand what you going through in order to be understanding. A person does not need have experienced depression in order to have a positive impact. Be open to that possibility.

90. Try to be picky about who you call your friend. There are billions of people in the world, many of whom speak the same language you do. You can set high standards for who you let into your life. Keep in mind that you can have different kinds of relationships in your life. Some people might make great acquaintances but not very good friends. Other people may seem like amazing people, but not the kind that you need in your life right now. This is okay.

91. Do not assume the future. Things change and are every so often unpredictable. Assumptions add stress. Assuming today is going to be awful when you have only been awake for a few minutes will probably not help you. Assuming tomorrow will be a bad before it gets here undoubtedly is not healthy. Keep an open mind about what the future may bring.

92. Everyone misses a mark. Part of the human experience is to learn from mistakes, missed opportunities, and mishaps. Mental illness might make rebounding from these situations difficult but keep in mind you are not the only one struggling. It is normal to reach for a goal and fall short the first time you try. Ask yourself what you learned from that experience and move forward.

93. It is okay to admit your feelings exist. You might be experiencing and feeling some bad stuff right now. It may help ease your suffering if you acknowledge that your feelings are valid. Write them down, talk to your medical professional about what you are experiencing, or simply remind yourself that they are real. It is not crazy to admit you exist and that your emotions exist. It is okay to confirm your moods. You might be the only one at this moment in time that can.

94. Do not assume you know what other people are thinking and feeling. You are unique and so is every other human on the planet. Every person experiences life in their own way. It is not appropriate to assume you can guess what someone is thinking or feeling. Their behavior or body language might provide clues, but instead of assuming, try asking. If he or she does not wish to share, do not pressure them. You can respect another person's privacy. You probably would want the same respect shown to you.

95. Respect other people's space. Every person has a right to private space, both physically and mentally. Each person may need or desire a different amount of privacy. Allow each person to choose what amount of privacy they want. Do your best to respect their decision. It may be hard, but put forth the effort let others set their own boundaries. It will help you form positive relationships with the people in your life.

96. You actually do need people. Let them help you. You are not expected to know everything about yourself or the illness that you are dealing with. Reach out and talk to people. Ask for help and seek out others who have experience overcoming similar problems. It may be hard for you to ask for help, but it is even harder to try to get well by yourself.

97. Do not obsess about cost. Medical care can get expensive, but disregard all of that right now. Today, right now, you need to just focus on getting well. If on that journey you need to spend money on your care, and then do so. You are important and your health is important. If it begins to add stress, consider creating a notebook or other type of space for these medical bills and notes. You may not be able to make the payments you would like, but you can organize the paperwork that debt is printed on.

98. You may find that your significant other cannot provide all the support you need. In most relationships, he or she cannot, which is why it is healthy to have friends and other types of people in your life. It does not mean you are needy or hard to handle. It means you are normal. It is okay to look outside of your closest relationships for extra support. You are not doing anything wrong if you want to make new friends, join a club, or get a second opinion. Just keep in mind what is appropriate for each type of relationship and strive to not to cross any boundaries.

99. Today is a good day for change. You do not have to wait for a holiday or special occasion to start making changes towards a healthier, more positive life. It is easy to make vague promises that at some point in the future you will start a new habit or attempt a new routine. You do not need to wait for the calendar to give you permission. You can give yourself permission to start today to make the changes you need to live healthier.

100. Appointments might feel like a waste of time, but go anyway. Not every appointment with a medical professional is going to feel productive, but try to attend every single one of them. Your doctor needs to see you regularly so he or she can gather all the information needed to provide you with the best care. You need the opportunity to communicate with those helping you what your most recent concerns are. Sometimes you want something to be fixed that is not fixable at this moment, but will be in the near future. It takes time and it takes your commitment to show up in order for these big changes to happen. It is okay if you miss one occasionally, but try to attend as many as you can.

101. It is okay to get a second opinion. Occasionally you passionately disagree with the advice your medical provider gave you. It is okay to disagree. It is also okay to ask another professional for a second opinion. You have the right as a patient to gather more information and try your best to make sure you are getting the best care available. Just keep in mind that there may be multiple valid ways to treat your symptoms, so if you find two professionals disagree, they may both be right. It is just that one person's advice is more useful to you, and that is okay.

102. You do not have to apologize for how you feel. Whether you are happy or sad, it does not matter. You do not need to feel any amount of shame for your emotions or say you are sorry for having them. You are you and if right now you are feeling an extreme mood, then so be it. Embrace and accept yourself by not apologizing when your feelings make you or someone else feel uncomfortable.

103. Treatments for clinical depression do not always have to include medications. You might be scared to talk about how much you are suffering. You may fear a pill is your only opinion, but it is not. There are different treatments available. It is okay to ask for alternatives. With each passing year, new knowledge and research creates more efficient ways of treating depression. Not every treatment plan requires that you take pills. Ask for help if you think you need it.

104. Taking a step back is not quitting or failure. It is okay and perfectly normal to step away from the current situation and look at the big picture. At times you may need to step back or reverse a decision so that you can move forward in a better direction. The path to a better, more healthy future is not going to be a constant road of improvement. You may encounter times when things are not working and that is okay. It is not a sign that improvement is not possible. You have done nothing wrong. You just might need to make a small change.

105. Seek out professional help early. The longer you live with symptoms of depression, the more severe it may become. You may also develop other health problems too. It will be easier to understand what kinds of help you need and to communicate accurately to help professionals what is happening inside your mind and body. As the illness grows in severity, you might have fewer choices in your health care and it may impact other aspects of your health. If you are able to, see a doctor as soon as you can if you believe you are experiencing symptoms or if your symptoms are getting worse.

106. Depression is not always about a type of sadness. People experience depression differently and their bodies may react differently. The experience may not involve tears and feelings of worthlessness. It may involve apathy or just otherwise you may feel you are not in touch with yourself. It may involve joint pain, muscle tension, fatigue, and other signs of physical stress. When in doubt, ask. It is better to speak up then discover later it may be something more serious.

107. It is also okay to take a break and relax for a short while. Taking time to rest is healthy. It often helps relieve stress and anxiety. Pausing for clarity is not a sign of giving up or failing. It is the action of a responsible person seeking a better way of life. There is no reason to feel guilty for taking a short break. You deserve it.

108. It is not shameful to have clinical depression. You may encounter people who will attempt to cause you embarrassment or treat you disrespectfully because you have a mental illness. You do not need that negativity so ignore the attempts. From time to time you have to be the bigger person and let it go. In time, hopefully more people will understand what depression is and is not, but today that is not your problem to take on. Just focus on you.

109. Periodically self-assess. It will probably take some time before you feel better, but it is good to have realistic expectations of progress. The order in which symptoms improve and the amount of relief you experience is hard to predict. Despite this, it is okay to assess your progress from time to time. If you are dissatisfied, think about giving other treatments or strategies a chance. You have the right to seek out improved care.

110. Attempt to identify what kind of support you need. Then ask for it. You might know exactly what you need in order to solve a problem by yourself. It is okay to ask for resources, support, and tools. Some might be more open to helping you solve a problem when you provide specific requests.

111. You may dream and desire whatever you want. Developing a severe medical condition may alter the timeline of achieving your dreams, but you have the freedom to dream whatever you want. Do not let anyone tell you that you cannot live the kind of life you want and desire. You deserve to be happy and to live a life you enjoy.

112. It is not your responsibility to make everyone around you happy. You may gain something from pleasing other people. It may be easier to please others than yourself, but it is not your responsibility to do so. You do not need to base your decisions on what will make others happy. You are allowed to make yourself happy. It is okay.

113. If you cannot do something right now, that is fine. Your current abilities will change with time as you continue to progress. Focus on making the most of what you are able to do right now. Contribute the most you can, give as much energy as you can, and give this moment your best. In time, you will have new skills and opportunities. You will be able to do more soon. Try your best to be patient with yourself.

114. You are probably going to get comfortable being uncomfortable. Sometimes clinical depression lasts so long that you may actually be more comfortable in that state than being healthy. Habits, even unhealthy ones, will become comfortable to you because they will be familiar. When you break old habits and move on to a healthier lifestyle, it will feel uncomfortable at first. Do not back off just because you are uneasy. You may be doing exactly what you need to in order to get better.

115. Practice being resilient. Things do not always go as planned and that is okay. Every time something does not go the way you want to, you have an opportunity to practice bouncing back. With time and repetition, it will be easier to rebound after a setback.

116. Speak up when you need something. Your needs may seem obvious to you, but they are usually not obvious to others. You will need to advocate for yourself when you need help. You likely will have to do this each and every time you need something. It requires a lot of energy and it may be very hard, but you can do it. You can speak up for yourself. Each time you do, it gets easier.

117. You can be nice and forgiving to you. Treat yourself with compassion and understanding. Sometimes the best person to give you the type of kindness you need is you. There is nothing wrong with that. The world has not failed you. Sometimes you are the best person for the job.

118. Celebrate your victories. All victories are important and so make an effort to celebrate them. Even small victories are worthy of praise. Give yourself credit when you have earned it, even for the little stuff. If it is important to you, then you should recognize it as such.

119. Avoid assigning value to everything. Let some people, things, and experiences just exist. You do not have to label everything as good or bad. Many things can appear and leave and just simply be a thing that was or is. It does not need your approval to exist. You can allow all kinds of people and experiences to cross your path without your energy reacting to them. It takes some practice, but it may be very freeing to not respond to all things that come in contact with your life.

120. Take back ownership of more of your time. There may be times during the week when you feel like you have turned over your life, but you have not. You may have to go to work, to an appointment, to run errands, but what you do on the journey there is your time. You can choose how you travel, the route of your trip, and what you do while making the journey. All of that is your time. You can choose how you spend it.

121. All you can realistically ask for is an opportunity. Try to look for and take advantage of opportunities to succeed. It may be appealing to look for large, glowing opportunities, but be open to more mundane ones as well. There are a lot of opportunities that appear small. When you take hold of them and use them, you usually will start to find success.

122. It might feel uncomfortable to experience joy again. Occasionally you may experience an odd occurrence where you can tell you are getting better, but you still feel uneasy. Doing things that make you happy may still feel weird. It might be the case that these feelings are actually now uncomfortable because it has been so long since you have felt them. That is okay. Keep making healthy choices and continue moving forward. In time, it will all feel comfortable again.

123. A little bit of acting may be required sometimes. That is okay. It is okay if you feel awful but you act happy long enough to run a quick errand or sit through a short meeting. You are probably not hurting yourself by doing this because it is good to practice what happy looks like and sounds like. You cannot do this for long periods of time because you will wear yourself out, but for very short periods of time, it is usually fine.

124. You can be true to yourself. It is possible to spend your time doing things you may not like but still be honest to yourself. Honestly does not mean telling every person every detail of your life. Being true to yourself means making decisions and committing to actions that will over time help you reach the goals you desire. As long as your daily actions are true to that, then you are being honest.

125. Consider getting rid of clutter. We all have extra stuff. Keep in mind there are more choices than the toss it or keep it options. Some things you can donate. Papers you can scan into your computer. Sometimes you can take a photo of something and that is just as good as the real thing. Having less stuff to keep track of may reduce your stress level. It might be challenging, but start small. Reducing your clutter may have a big positive impact.

126. Remove the word hate from your vocabulary. Try using the word 'dislike' instead. Have a go at using phrases like 'that did not appeal to me' or 'I do not enjoy that'. Even when you think, try to use a different word other than 'hate'. Removing that word from your daily vocabulary will start the process of seeing the world as the many shades of gray and colors that it is.

127. You can be open to change. There is a lot of truth to the idea that the only constant you can count on is change. Just as happy feelings go away and fun experiences end, the same is true for sad feelings and unhappy events. When life is good, be thankful. When your life is in some way disappointing, know that this too will change. In time, it will be different. Allow yourself to be open to that possibility.

128. Sometimes things do not go according to plan and that is okay. You can research and carefully list the best way to achieve something. You can do everything on your end perfectly, but yet it still does not turn out the way you want. It is a big world. There are things outside of your control. You are not a failure if something unexpected happens. You did nothing wrong.

129. Having suicidal thoughts does not mean you are permanently defective. If you were experiencing a heart attack, or a stroke, or started vomiting blood, you would seek out urgent medical care. You would probably go to your nearest emergency room. Suicidal thoughts are just as serious of a health condition and just as deserving of your urgent response. You are not broken beyond repair. You can be helped, you can get better, but first, you need to accept that this deserves immediate medical attention and seek it out right now.

130. Your perspective of reality is exclusive. Part of the human experience is to live a unique life with a unique perspective on reality. Reality is just a common meeting place, not a constant requirement. You will have moments that are real that others might not experience. There is no need to panic if for a moment you experience something unique.

131. You decide your purpose. There are many things in life you do not get to choose such as when the sun rises, where you were born, and why you blink. Your purpose and the purpose of all your experiences comes from your choice to define one. Creating a purpose begins with you and your commitment to establishing one.

132. You can do things by yourself. If something interests you, then go do it. You do not need to wait until you find someone to accompany you. You can see movies, take a walk, attempt a new recipe, start a new project, and do many more activities by yourself. It may be scary or uncomfortable the first few times, but if you are able, try doing something on your own.

133. Avoid abusing medicines. You may be suffering. It may seem to you that it is never ending. You may be frustrated. Using medicines in a manner other than prescribed is not a good way to handle the pain, nor is abusing over the counter medications. Your pain is temporary, but abusing medicines may actually prolong your suffering. Try practicing coping strategies, relaxation techniques, or positive self-talk. Make it a priority to talk to a medical professional if you feel that your current treatment plan is not working. Even when pain is the greatest, you have a lot of control over your long term outcome. You deserve a healthy way to manage your pain and suffering so ask for it, seek it out, and do not give up. Do not settle for quick fixes. You deserve better.

134. It is okay to talk about it. Bottling up emotions or concerns might actually be hurtful and add stress. Just keep in mind that other people in your life are not required to listen to you. At times a journal is helpful because some topics are best expressed in writing. If you really feel you need to speak aloud, then seriously think about working with a therapist. Not everything you are going through will be understood by your friends and loved ones. That is okay. No one has done anything wrong. No one has wronged you. You just need to be realistic about who can provide which kind of support.

135. You are never too old to dream a new dream. No matter how many years you have been on the planet, your age is in reality just a number. Live past this idea of a number and dream away. Set new goals, plan for new accomplishments, and begin taking action. You deserve to be as big of a dreamer as you want and set the goals you desire to achieve. You have that right, all you need to do is give yourself permission to experience and own your desires.

136. Two different opinions can both be right. Some scenarios or topics have no wrong answer, which means everyone is right. You can disagree with another and that does not mean that you are a lesser person or wrong in any way. It just means you have an equally valid, but different opinion.

137. It is okay to not be good at something. It is common to be good at some things and not so good at others. It is also common to learn quickly in one area, but not so quickly in another area. If it takes you more time than you would like to develop a skill, do not worry. It may just be a skill area where you need more time to mature. This does not mean you are broken, it just means you are a typical person. There is no shame in needing to work longer than you desire at a task. It happens. It is okay.

138. Let depression be its own identity, not your identity. Depression potentially may be for you a long lasting illness. In that time, you will grow and change. You would have grown and changed with or without depression, so it is sometimes hard to know what changes would have happened if you had not developed a severe medical condition. A good way to handle this uncertainty is to accept and love the entire current you. Treat yourself with kindness and compassion every second of every day. You existed first, depression came later. It will leave eventually, and you will remain. Part of your life story is that you developed clinical depression, not the other way around. Remember that you are bigger and more permanent than any illness.

139. There is not just winning and losing. Many people enter into a conversation or argument with the idea there are only two outcomes: to win or to loose. This is a very unhealthy way to view human interaction. There are many other outcomes. It is possible to enter into a discussion and for everyone to leave with all that they need. Focus on identifying what you need, how to most accurately communicate that need, and be open to meeting your need without fighting for it. Occasionally just asking is all that is required to get your needs met.

140. Avoid self-medicating. The path to recovery requires you to use your power to work towards a healthier you, which will become difficult if you choose to self-medicate. If you succumb to the temptation to attempt to self-medicate, what you are effectively doing is giving away your power. You are giving it to a drug, an emotionless, uncompassionate drug. It does not care about you or your health. The path to recovery requires you to use your power to work towards a healthier you. No substance will do that for you.

141. You are not damaged. You are not a person of lesser value because you have a medical condition. You are no less important no matter what happens to you. Things will happen that are outside of your control, but none of them impact your worth. You are still a human being of full value.

142. Consider removing the phrase 'should have' from your vocabulary. Telling yourself that you should have done this or that implies that you are now less human because you were unable to do this thing you told yourself you simply 'should' do. Instead, describe your desired actions as things you want to do or something that you would like to do. There are many ways to express or think about your intentions.

143. There is an unlimited amount of good in the universe. You do not need to hurt someone else in order to feel happy or gain goodness. You can achieve your goals, have good things happen to you, or simply experience something positive without stealing it or taking from somewhere else. There is not some kind of hidden balance that must be maintained in order for reality to exist. It is okay to feel happy, take part in pleasing events and relationships, or otherwise experience joy.

144. Anger usually exists atop other emotions. Anger is connected to other emotions like disappointment or sadness. It is often rooted in other feelings. Before assuming that the only emotion you have towards something is anger, stop. Ask yourself what else you are feeling. You are possibly feeling something else, which is more fundamental to the problem. Therefore, if you resolve that underlining emotion, the anger will often also start to resolve.

145. There is probably more you can do in your relationships. Before assuming that other parties are to blame in your relationships, take a hard look at your actions. There may be more you can do. Do not trivialize the small stuff. The only person you can control in any relationship is you. If you can do more, then do so. If you cannot, then perhaps you need to change the relationship, or leave it.

146. It is okay to be ungrateful. You do not have to love the present you received. You do not have to find the help given useful. It is fine if you really are not appreciative of what some else does for you. It is most certainly a good idea to still thank the person for their time, their hard work, or their effort, but you by no means owe anyone your full gratitude.

147. Give the people in your life a break. If someone is unable to provide the support you need, be forgiving. If someone has provided advice based on bad information, be compassionate. You may desire a kind of support they are not capable of giving. A person can love you and care about you, but just not be able to provide the kind of support you desire right now. That is okay. Try to accept people as they are and forgive.

148. Change is not going to ask for your permission. Each day brings new opportunities and new circumstances. These are not going to wait for your approval to happen. It might be scary, but it is also exciting. Be open to unexpected change and do your best to remain flexible and resilient.

149. Some things may need to stay a private matter. Stop and consider how it is best to express what you are going through. Maybe writing in a journal is best. Maybe keeping some things between you and one other trusted individual is best. While it is okay to get it out in the open, you probably need to be selective about how you do it. It is okay if someone in your life does not want to hear about an aspect of your suffering. They have the right to not listen just as you have the right to want to speak. You can process privately. You have that power and ability to do so.

150. Sadness and depression are different. Sadness is a healthy emotion that everyone experiences at some point in their lives. While experiencing depression, you may feel a prolonged version of this healthy emotion, but sadness in itself is not necessarily bad. Some times in life, feeling sad may be the healthiest way to react to something that has happened to you. If you experience sadness and then you are able to move forward there is no reason to panic.

151. Practice being fully present in the here are now. Being more aware of this moment will help decrease stress by limiting the amount of energy you are devoting to other moments of time and space. You deserve to experience your life in its fullest. One way is to focus on this current instant and be aware of it in its entirety. Acknowledgment of this moment of time, even if parts of it are negative to you, might help.

152. Personal passions are found through action. The best way to discover your talents is by doing things. Try something new that you think you might like. It is difficult to know if you will enjoy something unless you actually do it. Thinking about it, talking about it, and even planning for it are all very limiting. When you take on the responsibility of action you are actually experiencing your desires. Through the experience of action you can more clearly define what drives and motivates you.

153. Make exercising fun. Select activities that you enjoy doing. You are probably more likely to develop a new healthy habit if you find the activity pleasurable. Try new things and be open to new ways of getting up and moving. If it is difficult to find delight in any style of movement, attempt the simple act of doing something new. A novel experience may seem worthy of your time. Avoid the temptation to create expectations about how your body should react to the exercising and just focus on the commitment to be active.

154. Give yourself time to heal. Your body is not designed to repair itself instantly. No amount of willpower is going to change this fact. In a culture filled with expectations of instant gratification and solutions, this might be frustrating for you. Practice being patient, be kind and forgiving to your body as it is recovering, and do not give up hope.

155. Schedule self-care and downtime. You can create the time to take care of yourself. You deserve to have moments when you can relax. Plan time you can devote only to self-care, even if it is only a few minutes. Commit to a schedule of regular periods of downtime when you can relax. A few minutes of deep breathing, a few stretches, a quiet minute in a place you feel comfortable mostly likely will reduce stress.

156. Remember to eat. When learning to cope with a serious illness, it is easy to simply forget to eat. Try actually scheduling time for eating meals. Try to eat at the same time each day. Stock up easy to make snacks that are healthy and try to maintain a balanced diet. Talk to a medical professional if you believe you may need to supplement your diet with any vitamins. A regular pattern of healthy eating most certainly will help you feel better.

157. Do the most you can with what you have. Think about reevaluating how you are using the resources you currently have access to. You may find that you can do more just by making small changes with the current tools at your disposal. You may not need all the stuff you yearn for. There often are many ways to get to a destination or goal, so keep an open mind and reevaluate what you have. With practice, being more efficient and resourceful will become habit.

158. Consider joining a club or taking a class. An excellent way to meet people is to try new activities. One way to make a go at new things is to join a club or take a class. Research what is available in your area. There often are inexpensive offerings through city or state sponsored programs. Ask for help if you struggle to find something that might interest you. There are also a lot of classes online, some are for free. Taking a class online may potentially be helpful, but sometimes classes where you meet people in person are better. It often is easier to meet new people and talk to them when you can see them face to face.

159. Embrace and love you as you are. There is no need to wait until the future to accept the entire you. You can practice random thoughts of kindness towards yourself in the present moment. Accept yourself as you are, let go of any expectations that only if you were different you would be worthy of such praise. You deserve to be loved by you, so take a break from any negative self-talk and give yourself some admiration.

160. Take a look at the whole picture. Avoid letting one small event ruin an otherwise very good day. Everything may go as planned and then you encounter a snag, a small wrinkle, a tiny event that potentially could offset you, but do not let it. Let go of the small stuff and focus on the bigger event that is your day, your week, and your life. You are not a failure if one small mistake or unpredictable mishap occurs.

161. Avoid creating excuses for good things that happen. Not every good thing that goes your way is just a coincidence. Try resisting temptation to diminish the goodness. You deserve to have good things happen in your life. You may have earned the positive outcome, or it happened as a result of hard work or good planning, so try to enjoy it.

162. Feeling bad is only that, nothing more. Try not to assume that feeling bad somehow means that you are bad, life is bad, or that reality is bad. Your feelings exist and fluctuate independently, so respect them as such.

163. You are more than a single event or decision. Avoid giving yourself labels based on a single mistake or a one-time shortcoming. Self-imposed negative labels originating out of these single instances may create a further stress and anxiety. You are far too valuable to shortchange with such labels.

164. Practice healthy sleep habits. It may take time, but work towards sleeping the same amount each night. Strive to limit your naps during the day and when you wake up, get up. The longer you linger in bed, often the harder it is to get moving and maintain energy.

165. Forgive yourself. You have the power to forgive yourself for anything and everything. Your forgiveness is just as strong, if not more important. You can decide to discontinue the blame, the disappointment, and the resentment that you may be holding on to. It is not serving you, so let it go and replace it with more positive thoughts, opinions, and feelings.

166. Stop trying and just start letting more be. It is possible to obsess about getting well and recovering. It is possible to expect results too fast. Some symptoms are not going to go away faster than your body can heal itself and no amount of talking, reading, or discussing can expedite things. It is good to desire progress and it is good to be willing to work, but do not overdo it. Find a healthy balance.

167. It is okay to distract yourself. Every now and then the only thing you can do to provide some relief is to direct your attention away from your pain and suffering by taking up a small project. Completing a jigsaw puzzle, a painting, reading a book, watching a movie, or any other similar activity will help. In a short time, your body will feel different, maybe not completely relieved, but better.

168. Let go of the idea of a perfect person. There is no such thing as being perfect. Setting high expectations for you can lead to a lot of unhealthy behavior and negative self-talk. Instead, focus on creating realistic expectations and goals. If you make a mistake, do not allow it to smear your self-worth or diminish your value. Try to not aim for perfection, instead aim for being the healthiest you in your power to create.

169. Spend time being honest about how you view the negative. Do not give negativity more weight than it deserves. Acknowledge its existence, but spend more of your time and energy acknowledging the positive. If you struggle with this, write down negative thoughts as you think them and share your notes with a medical professional. Too much obsession on negativity might begin to hurt your progress towards recovery.

170. Avoid trying to stop behaviors. Instead, replace them with healthier habits. Your behavior is serving some kind of a need, so when you discontinue it without another behavior in its place to meet that need, you will start to suffer. All that extra suffering will result in your inability to maintain your goal to discontinue the bad habit. Focus on the addition of more positive ways of acting and being. Consider taking the time to identify what need that unhealthy habit is serving and practice a better way of living to achieve the same end.

171. Write about what you like most. One exercise that may help relieve you of negativity is to write about what you believe to be your best quality. If it is hard to write about yourself, try instead writing about a topic you enjoy. If nothing comes to mind, then write about something new that you have not explored before and therefore have no feelings towards yet. Explore the thought, describe it. Discuss your unique viewpoint on the matter.

172. Explore an obsession. One way to try to get rid of an obsession is to make it boring by writing about it until you have mentally explored every possible avenue of its existence. It may fill whole journals, but it might be worth a try if other attempts of freeing your brain have failed. When you have finally become bored with this thought, think about destroying the pages you have written it on. Burning them or sending them through a paper shredder might be extremely satisfying and freeing.

173. Our problems are unique, so are our solutions. What works for someone else might not work for you. That is okay. You do not have the find the same pieces of advice useful, the same religious practices uplifting, or experience the same kind of happiness. It is okay to seek out solutions that work best for you.

174. Give back when you can. It may be difficult on occasion, especially when you are in great pain, but attempt to give to others when you can. Taking the time and energy to help another person will help you reconnect with the world around you and it just might leave you feeling better.

175. Create a physical space that is your retreat. You may benefit from spending some time in a calm space where you feel emotionally and mentally safe. You can create this space and go to it when you need to regroup and recharge. Create a corner with your favorite chair and lamp, put up pictures that make you smile, or maybe a quiet spot with a cup of tea is all you need. Make it personal, make it real. Retreat on a regular basis and give yourself permission to relax.

176. You have five senses, not all are equal. You may have times when one of your senses is causing you grief. Ignore it and focus on another. If hearing music and noises brings you pain, consider retreating to a quiet place and knitting, take on a craft project, or practice meditation. It is okay if you need to give one of your senses a break. You are not broken, you just need to focus on your needs and take care of yourself.

177. Rejections are just missed opportunities. You may provide someone with an opportunity and he or she chooses not to take advantage of it. You may feel rejected, but in reality you were not rejected. Instead, your opportunity was passed upon. Others have the right to not take advantage of your opportunities, just as you have the right to say no too. Someone may not want to be your friend, your date, or your partner in crime. That is okay, let others be. You are not a person of lesser worth because your offer was not accepted.

178. Do not pick fights with your thoughts. Allow your thoughts to exist and flow. When you try to be extremely abrasive to your own mind, your mind most likely will attempt to fight back. It is okay if you need to take a couple of seconds to let a thought run its course in your head to its end. When the thought is over it is easier to let it go, dismiss it, or ignore it.

179. Your presence is powerful. Simply showing up to the current moment and giving it your full attention is a very power way of being. You can impact the present moment a great deal, even your mindset may have a huge impact. A positive attitude can go a long way to achieving a positive moment of time for you to experience.

180. No need to apply logic to feelings. You may want to apply a reason or understand why you are experiencing a certain emotion. Try not to find a reason, just let your emotions exist and be. Let yourself be. The intensity will pass, your emotions will pass. Try to exist with your emotions without judgment.

181. Define success by your own terms. You get to decide what is most important to you and therefore which achievements are the most notable. You have the power to decide what your achievements look like and feel like. When you have reached a goal, celebrate your success.

182. Take the time to define your goals. Ambiguous goals rarely get achieved because you most likely do not know what it would look like and feel like to achieve them. Make it a priority to describe and define your goals. Describe all the steps you need to take in order to reach your goals and celebrate each step of victory along the way.

183. Challenges may show up more than once. You have not failed if a problem shows up in your life more than once. Every so often a symptom will seem to have finally gone away only to make an unwanted appearance again later. Not all is lost. Do not give up hope because you may have to tackle a problem again. You are entering into the situation wiser this time around, so you are stronger this time too.

184. Failure is not the opposite of success. Actually, it is often part of success. The road to accomplishment is not straight and steep. On occasion really good attempts will completely fail fabulously. Learn from them. Carry that vast knowledge with you forward onto greater ways doing things.

185. Choose to be your own cheerleader. Give yourself compliments when you need them. It is not weird, it is a smart way to practice positive self-talk. When you expect others to give you the compliments you crave, you are waiting for someone else's permission to enjoy your life. Do not wait on others to bring joy into your day. You have the power to praise yourself.

186. Find a balance between acceptance and desire. It is great to practice self-acceptance. Loving your current self is a wonderful way to combat the seemingly constant bombardment of depressive symptoms, but there is a limit. If you find that your acceptance of the current here and now reaches extreme apathy, you might need to speak to your doctor or therapist. Constant apathy in itself may be a sign of concern that needs medical attention.

187. Fight issues and problems, not people. When discussing a conflict or if in the middle of an argument, focus on the issue at hand. Try to avoid bringing up past emotions or arguments. Resist the urge to engage in name calling. Focus on the current discussion and devote effort to simply resolving the issue at the heart of the matter.

188. Make an effort to keep short to-do lists. When your to-do list is long, it may be hard to focus on seeing a task to completion. Instead, try keeping two lists. One list could be your long term goals. The second list could be much shorter, just a few items, and reference the shorter list daily. Once you finish a task, you can celebrate your accomplishment and then add a new goal. Narrowing your focus in this manner can also help with anxiety and may reduce stress.

189. Go to bed at the same time each night. This may be difficult if you have a busy schedule, but attempt to make it a priority to so. Issues with sleep often are one of the most common symptoms of clinical depression and one of the hardest to resolve. A bedtime often helps establish a sleep schedule, but if sleep issues persist seriously consider talking to a medical professional for more personalized advice.

190. You can only give one hundred percent. Once you have maxed out your attention and energy, then that is it. There does reach a point in a situation where you are doing everything that you can. When living these moments, validate your hard work and your effort. Tell yourself that you truly are giving it your all and do not be too hard on yourself.

191. Productive and busy are often two different things. Both consume lots of your time and energy. When having a bad day, either is good, because they both help you cope. However, when looking at the big picture and long term goal planning, you want to strive to be productive and not just busy. You want to eventually develop habits that lead you to finishing tasks and projects because this will help you stay healthy.

192. Strive to do better today than you did yesterday. Long term planning may seem overwhelming. Problems that span days and weeks may add lots of stress to your life. Focus on and care more about how you are doing today compared to yesterday. You have the power to do small things right now that will help make today a better day.

193. Changes to your behavior will help change your brain. You must commit to changing behavior, including thoughts, before expecting your brain to operate differently. Often, there is a delay in the brain's response. Forming a new habit might take a few weeks, but it will almost certainly take still more time for the brain to respond to your hard work. Keep up your efforts and try your best not to panic, worry, or get discouraged.

194. Logic is a great way to self-check on a limited basis. Your emotions probably do not happen logically and that is okay. If you love logic, use it, but only to assess other aspects of yourself. Ask if your goals and expectations are logical and realistic. Do your best to let your emotions be.

195. Identify your stressors outside of depression. You may have stress triggers that are draining you of your energy that are not caused by your severe medical condition. You likely can reduce your stress level by making it a priority to change the way you respond to these triggers. Sometimes they are not your biggest causes of stress, but tackling even the small stuff can improve your well-being.

196. Schedule positive events. You can prioritize positive happenings by setting aside time for them in your schedule. It may be difficult to give these the same value as other obligations, but make the choice to do things for you. You deserve positive experiences and interactions. They may not always make you happy, but positive events will help you be healthy.

197. Minimize comparing yourself and your life to others. It is okay to observe another person or their life for a few moments, but do not determine your life's value based on that comparison. It is by taking action, living your own life, and determining your self-worth independently of any outside event will you most likely achieve the healthiest life in your power to create.

198. Select a realistic short-term goal daily. Each day, set a goal for you to achieve by the time the day is done. Focus on achieving this goal. Initially, pick something which takes only a few minutes of time to complete. In time, once you have gotten in the habit of daily goal setting, select slightly longer goals. Remember to give yourself credit for the victory, even in a small way like crossing your achieved goal off your to-do list.

199. Create a healthy sleeping space. Do your best to create an environment where you sleep that is free of extra lights and noises. Avoid reading, watching movies or television, and eating while in bed. Try changing the side you sleep on or the direction you sleep. Maybe facing away from a window might work for you or maybe you sleep better wearing socks to bed. You will not know until you try different ways of organizing your sleeping space, so practice making this a priority.

200. It is okay if you are not in the mood to do something. This is not a sign that you are getting worse or are otherwise not well. At times you simply just do not feel like doing something and if you begin to read more into it than that you will only add unwanted stress to your life. Practice accepting the current you as you are in this moment. Even accept that sometimes you will not be in the mood to do some things and that is fine.

201. Make sure you are showing up to social commitments. It is one thing to physically appear at an event, but another to also mentally and emotionally appear as well. Do your best to be fully present in all of your relationships with others, even the casual one-time interactions with strangers. It likely will help you feel more connected and in time you will find these interactions more fulfilling.

202. Try to connect with others over positive shared circumstances. You may meet new people who share in your pain and sorrows, but also attempt to connect with people who share your dreams or aspirations. Surrounding yourself with relationships formed out of positive connections may help your progress towards recovery and create an overall more healthy social life.

203. Practice being true to yourself. Being honest about your opinions, beliefs, and needs will help separate you from the symptoms of the illness. It will also help you attract people into your life that have similar interests and desires. It might be scary for you, but it takes a lot less energy to simply be honest.

204. Consider the benefits of documenting your feelings. Recording your emotions may provide you with some good information. It may help you understand the patterns of your mood swings so that you can avoid triggers and know in which environments you feel the best.

205. Intense feelings happen sometimes. It is okay to experience an extreme emotional reaction to some thing or event. When living with clinical depression, emotions may seem nonexistent and this causes numbness. They may also seem overdramatized and cause an intense emotional state. Both extremes may happen while you are dealing with any mental illness. Practice coping strategies until the feelings subside and resist any urges to attempt to use willpower to make yourself better. Willpower does not cure severe medical conditions. If your symptoms are bothersome, speak to your medical professional for additional help.

206. Budget both your time and your money. Make a budget and stick to it. It is wise to enter into a store with a list of needed items and to refrain from extra purchases. Try to treat your time as a currency of which you have a limited amount to use. Schedule and budget it wisely to strive to use it in the most efficient way possible. Prioritizing these kinds of purchases help rethink your wants and needs, which may help reduce stress and anxiety.

207. You might need to react emotionally to something more than once. It is okay and typical to need to emotionally respond to an event, person, or memory several times before being at a place where you can let it go for good. Avoid negative self-talk or forming the opinion that you are somehow broken if you need to express the same feelings again. Try writing in a journal or finding a healthy outlet for the emotions. Relying on other people to listen repeatedly may be too difficult for them, so explore other healthy outlets for your repeated emotional experiences. It is a valid need, treat it as such.

208. It is okay to say no. You may pass on opportunities when you need to. If a commitment would drain you of your energy, it might be best to pass on the chance for the experience. It is a big world with a lot of opportunities for you. It is okay to let a few pass by because they are not a good fit for you right now.

209. Remember to take breaks. While there are specific aspects of the treatment of a severe medical condition that you should never take a break from such as taking medication, eating, or sleeping. It is healthy to take breaks from other responsibilities, especially long lasting commitments. If you are able to take a break at work, do so. If you need an extra minute before walking in the front door, take an extra lap around the block first. Take a day off from your hobby. Take an hour off from constantly thinking positively. Give yourself a few minutes to just breathe and relax. Find a way to take a breather, a rest. You deserve it.

210. Explore a possible connection between stress and pain. For many, but not all, there may be things in your daily life that are acting as triggers for stress. There may even be some that result in an increase level of physical pain. You are not crazy, it may be connected. Think about taking the time and effort to identify any stress triggers. Attempt to limit exposure to those triggers. If that is not possible, consider alternative ways of perceiving the stress or practice different ways of responding to it. You may want to speak to your doctor or therapist if you are unable to find a healthy way to reduce exposure to such triggers after you identify them.

211. Try routine stretching or yoga. When creating a morning or bedtime routine, think about including something to help relax your body. A few minutes of simple stretching may not feel good immediately, but it may be a small way to have a big impact on your day or your night's sleep.

212. You probably are not a lifelong sufferer of depression. There are many different types of depression. Not all cases of depression will last for years and you do not know how long exactly your illness will last. Do not let the stigma or stereotype that you have to be a life-long suffer of the illness deter you from your progress. Continue working on creating a healthier you.

213. Listen to your body. Pay attention to warning signs. You know your body better than anyone, so take it seriously. If you know that something does not feel right, make it a priority to help yourself. You can readjust your schedule to allow more self-care, you may attempt to get a little bit more sleep, or perhaps you need to speak to a medical professional. You are your body's first line of defense, so trust your instincts. If your body is telling you something, try to pay attention.

214. View frustration as an opportunity to practice patience.
Events will happen outside of your control, but you can choose to form any opinion your wish. You may choose to be frustrated, adding to your emotions. You may also choose to see these events as opportunities to practice being patient without letting anxiety build inside of you. Practice different ways to calm yourself into a less anxious state. Take a deep breath, refocus your attention, and strive to gain a new perspective. You deserve to be less anxious and stressed. Invest in the effort to regain a better, healthier state of being.

215. Stay away from and out of gossip. You may go to the source of the story or simply ignore it if you wish to find peace faster. Repeating stories based on hearsay or talking about people while they are not present may add stress to your life. You are devoting energy and focus to something that probably will not improve your health or aid in your recovery. Make an effort to remain silent if gossip comes up in conversation. In time, the topic will change and you can contribute again.

216. Take care of yourself first. It may be hard to put yourself first, but you likely will feel less stressed if you make your wellbeing a priority. There is no need to self-indulge, but by investing a little more energy into your own health, you will have more energy to devote to the wellbeing of those around you. In a big way, helping yourself will often help others.

217. Wake up at same time every day. Do your best to wake up each day at the same time. If you feel that you need extra sleep, try going to bed an hour earlier. Sleeping in might negatively influence your energy level for the rest of the day. Consider developing the habit of a wake up routine too. In time, a set morning schedule might ease your suffering and stress level.

218. There is an existence beyond you. Some may call this a higher power, but you may call it whatever you wish. Having an understanding that there is some kind of entity beyond you will probably help you recover. Accepting that you are not the center of it all helps put you into a healthier, more grounded viewpoint of reality. You are part of a greater whole of some sort. Its name, the exact nature of your relationship with it is all up to you. Finding peace with your beliefs regarding your relationship with life outside of your existence is something you have the power to do.

219. Review your journals and notes. Periodically look for patterns in your writings. You may discover that there are patterns to your thoughts and habits. These patterns might provide you with new awareness. Clinical depression can be complex and recovery from it may require a combination of different types of treatment. Any new perspective you may gain from your own writings might greatly aid in your recovery.

220. It is alright to not know what you need for your future. You will not know everything you want to know or feel you need to know and that is okay. You can make goals and work towards a better future without knowing everything. It may be scary, but you can create the life you want and make changes without having everything figured out beforehand.

221. Right now, you are a different person than you were. You have changed already. You will continue to change more. The person you will be in the future will be different than who you are now or ever were. You are many different people in one lifetime. Use the knowledge that you have acquired to work towards recovery. May the person you are creating through all your hard work, the future you, be wiser for it.

222. Self-care does not need to be productive. At times self-care is all about recovery, self-preservation, or just monitoring. There is no need to pressure yourself into setting goals while you are trying to relax. You do not need to be productive or achieve anything while you are experiencing some down time. Just be kind to yourself and try to unwind.

223. Do not waste your energy on fighting history. Allow the past to remain in the past. Resist the temptation to bring up past emotions and conflict into current arguments. Focus your energy and time on the present. Allow yourself the freedom to just be responsible for this current moment in time.

224. You are not missing. There is no need to go looking for you. You do not need to find yourself. You are here and are living in this moment. What needs to happen is that you need to spend effort creating the future you that you wish to become.

225. Try new things. It may be scary, but try something new. Go to a new park, take a new route, taste a new food. In time, it will become easier. New experiences often help keep the brain and body healthy. Start with a level that feels comfortable and work towards trying new things that might result in you meeting new people. Social interactions centered on topics new to you may also help you grow and become healthier.

226. Accept real life examples that may contradict your worldview. Strive to live each day according to beliefs you have formed based on real life examples that you can specifically recall. Accept the challenge that new life experiences may affect your way of seeing the world. It is okay to allow your viewpoint of life to be influenced by specific real events. If you feel moved by a piece of music, or great food, or a stunning sunset there is no need to dismiss it. Your worldview is in flux and will grow, just like you.

227. You may still face difficulties after doing all the right stuff. There is no guarantee that by doing everything in your power to do that you will reach your goals without any kind of difficulty. Realistically, you probably will have some difficulties. However, resist the urge to stop. Press forward and onward. Keep doing what you need to do to build a life you are proud of. The path to a healthier life may be filled with an unfair share of misfortune, but that does not mean you are doing anything wrong or that you are a failure. Keep doing what is right for you.

228. You do not need to believe everything you think. Some thoughts may need to just pass through your mind and disappear. Not everything you come up with is useful or healthy. Focus on your power to choose what thoughts to give value to and which to dismiss. Select ideas that empower you, that reaffirm your connection to reality, or that aid you in a similar way.

229. It is okay to be lost while traveling in the right direction.
There is no need to insist that you know every detail of your journey.
As long as you are moving forward in the general direction that you
need to end up, then it is fine. Allow today to be detailed and
specific, but refrain from obsessing about needing that same level of
detail about your distant future.

230. Think about how another sees you. Imagine your current
situation from someone else's perspective, like a seven year old
child, a dog, or cat. Understanding how your life events may be
interpreted by someone else may provide a little bit of clarity when
you feel overwhelmed, stressed, or anxious.

231. Create something tangible. Set aside time to make or build
something that you can finish in a short amount of time. Do
something small so that you can feel and experience what it is like to
finish something that you begin. Celebrate your results and enjoy
your creation.

232. Set out to meet new people. It is okay to take up a hobby or
attend events with the intent to meet new people. Just remember that
it takes time to develop a friendship, so start small. Greet people and
invest in the energy to engage in small talk.

233. You may need to modify your beliefs and that is okay. You
may need to rethink your worldview a few times while you progress
through treatment. You might experience some things that challenge
your understanding of the world. It is normal and healthy to allow
your personal experiences to alter your understanding of the

universe. It is not a sign of going crazy, but a sign of responsibly. You are adjusting to your current self and life.

234. Keep a food and medicine diary. If you choose to take medication, it is important to take the medicine as directed for as long as you are advised to by medical professionals. Keeping a diary recording everything you eat, including when you take medications, can help you stay healthy. Sometimes a treatment plan is complicated and it is difficult to remember when to take the medication, so keeping a food and medicine diary may help. Also, consider sharing the information contained in your diary with your doctor so that he or she can better assist you.

235. The treatment is unfair. Often the type of treatment required comes with side effects or drawbacks that you unfortunately experience before experiencing any benefits. This is unfair and possibly cruel. However, you have the strength to stick to the treatment plan you select. Enduring side effects for a short while is worth the long term trade off of good health in your future.

236. You are beautiful and lovely. Being you is a wonderful experience. Today, you may feel bad, but being you is great. Stop and appreciate your uniqueness as beautiful. Question your negative thoughts about your body. Ponder the possibility that unhealthy messages may come from outside sources. Love your entire self because regardless of your body's current condition, you always have been and always will be beautiful.

237. Ask your medical professionals questions regarding your treatment. It is okay to ask your doctor questions. Keep asking questions until you understand your treatment plan and why you are trying to follow it. Take notes so that when you get home, it is easier to remember what you are trying to do and why. You deserve to be an active part of your health care.

238. Refrain from thinking about what to say next. When in conversation, try not to think ahead by rehearsing in your mind what you want to say. Instead, focus on the person you are speaking with. Give him, or her, your undivided attention. Doing so will often help you listen better, which is a good skill to develop. It will likely help you create healthier relationships.

239. Take notes about your visits with medical professionals. It might be a good idea to express your feelings after you visit with a doctor or therapist, but it is even more helpful to simply take down the information that was exchanged during your visit. Try summarizing what was discussed and any instructions that were given. Accounts of the visit not weighed down by emotional reaction will greatly aid in your recovery because it can provide a reference for you to go to when you need to remember details.

240. You do not need to connect every conversation back to you. It is okay to just listen when someone is speaking without interjecting a story about your own life that is similar. It is not necessary to identify with every individual you encounter either. It is okay to have social interactions where you allow a person to tell you his whole story so you can truly get to know him and hear what he has to say.

241. Practice paraphrasing. A great skill to develop is paraphrasing or summarizing. You state in your own words what was just stated in conversation. It allows to you communicate that you are actually listening and gives you the opportunity to make sure that you are getting all the information accurately. You may accidently mishear something or get distracted. Paraphrasing allows you check into the social interaction in a way that does not require you to open up, which may feel safer and cause less anxiety.

242. Keep part of you private. It is okay to have part of yourself remain secret to just you. You are allowed that kind of privacy. Just remember to share with medical professionals what they need to know in order to help you, because withholding that kind of information may hinder your recovery and growth process. However, you can have private experiences and keep them to yourself. There is no need to share every thought with the outside world.

243. You do not have a direct relationship with the world. Your understanding of reality comes via your senses of sight, sound, touch, smell, and taste. Together, they help you form an understanding of reality, your personal worldview. There are things that might get in the way of you using your senses to get as accurate an understanding as is physically possible, but do not get frustrated if you disagree with others on the details. Just focus on maintaining as accurate of a worldview as you can, remembering that there is no such thing as perfect understanding.

244. A change my feel gradual, sudden, or be inconsistent. You may feel that a change is negative, often called a symptom, or positive, which is progress towards a kind of normalcy. You may feel that a negative change happened suddenly and was intense. These are good characteristics of your experiences to identify and communicate to those helping you. Your choice of words is very important. Taking the time to select adjectives like gradual, sudden, dull, or intense may help you obtain care that is the best fit for your needs.

245. You are being asked to take a leap of faith. You are not crazy for questioning different aspects of your mental health plan. There is no test to determine exactly what you need to get better, so some parts of your treatment may not work the first time. It is okay if you feel frustrated because you are being asked to trust a plan that may have some minor flaws that need revisiting. Only in time and with your complete compliance will you and those helping you develop your best treatment plan.

246. Make your home safe for you. You can make it a priority to remove items from your own home that may harm you including infrequently used sharp objects, unused medications, and any unnecessary tools. If your condition gets worse or is severe, give serious thought to boxing up items and giving them to a trusted friend or family member to hold on to at their house until you feel better. You really do not need extra pairs of scissors, nail clippers, razors, etc. at your home while you are recovering.

247. Refrain from exaggerating or lying to medical professionals. When you choose to withhold important information or lie about your symptoms, you likely are making your condition worse. Doctors and therapists are only capable of providing quality care with your cooperation. When you lie or withhold information, you are preventing yourself from getting the best care possible. You deserve high quality care, so try your best to communicate accurate information.

248. You do not need to let the diagnosis limit your future. You are allowed to dream whatever you wish. You may desire any future you can think of. Your only limitations are the laws that maintain the safety of the community we all live in and share. Give yourself permission to design a life around your passions and to keep seeking that which motivates you.

249. Practice good eye contact with others. You are still able to maintain, with a little bit of work, a lot of your communication skills throughout your recovery. However, you may need to work a little harder. Actions that came naturally may require some effort. Eye contact is a simple way to show you are engaged in your conversations.

250. Frequently seek out evidence of your beliefs. As you grow and change, parts of your belief system or world view might not be serving you anymore. You may also form very strong beliefs based on your feelings around specific people, things, or environments. Being open to obtaining information that validates your beliefs. Questioning your extreme emotional reactions may build confidence.

251. It is okay if you want something clarified. When something is confusing or you feel you do not have all the information, know that you have the power to understand by seeking out better knowledge. Not understanding something the first time does not mean you are dumb or a bad listener, it just means that you need to seek out different information. There is nothing wrong with that.

252. Commit to day of positivity. For one whole day, only post and say positive things on social media sites. Only spend time with people and in environments that give you energy. Avoid things that drain you and refrain from making negative comments. You might be surprised how well a small amount of goodness can transform your mood.

253. Clinical depression is more than a mood or an emotion. It is a severe medical illness. Just as you would seek out medical care for a broken bone, stroke, or diabetes, you probably should see a doctor if you think you have clinical depression. It is not a condition that you can control with prayer, wishful thinking, or positive thoughts.

254. Try fighting urges with distraction. You may find yourself overwhelmed by any number of distressing or obsessive ideas. If this happens, aim to distract your mind with an activity. Try watching a new movie, listening to a new song, or even organizing something in your room in a new way. You can pass a lot of time with different types of distraction. Distracting yourself away from severe symptoms might be the best way to cope right now and that is okay.

255. It is okay to not like someone. You do not have to love every single person you meet. There are billions of people on the planet. Odds are you might not like some of them. That is fine. What is not okay is disrespecting people or allowing your dislike to grow into hate. Give yourself permission to admit you might not like everyone, knowing that you can continue to be kind and compassionate to all.

256. Watch your tone when speaking. You communicate a lot with the volume and type of pitch of your voice. A whisper communicates meaning and so does shouting. Even if you spoke the exact same words, each level of tone adds more meaning to what you are trying to say. Be mindful of everything you are expressing when you speak.

257. Remember why you started. There is a reason you reached out for help in the first place. If you find that you are overwhelmed, remember your reason for starting treatment. Maybe you can now think of other reasons why you are attempting to make your life better. Continue to work towards a healthier you. Persist with your efforts to make your life more enjoyable. Reconnecting with your motivation may help you carry that purpose forward to the present and with you into the immediate future.

258. Medical treatment cannot cure unhappiness. Clinical depression, like all mental illnesses, is a severe medical condition that affects your physical body. The goal of your medical treatment is to make your physical body well again by assisting in its physical recovery. Your treatment can help repair you so you are capable of feeling happiness. Often, it is only through a combination of your actions, attitudes, and beliefs that happiness will start to appear in your life.

259. Ask people about their training. It is always okay to ask medical professionals about their experience and education. You have the right to understand this about your doctor or therapist's background. You may gain a better understanding of their point of view and develop more trust in their opinions. Having an increased respect for those helping you will probably reduce your anxiety about receiving treatment.

260. Focus on possibilities, not problems. You may get distracted by problems and the stress they ignite in your life. Take a step back from all of that and look at the possibilities that are in your life right now. Devote energy to moving towards those possibilities and making them a part of your life.

261. Commit to resolving conflict in a positive way. There are healthy ways to deal with conflict. It is not about always being on top, but rather how to handle the stress and create solutions that will improve the lives of all involved. Focus more on resolving one conflict at a time and stay in the present moment. There is no need to bring up old disagreements or drag more than one problem into the discussion. You deserve to improve your life through conflict resolution in a manner that does not add more stress to your life.

262. You can be your own hero. There is no need to look outside of you to find a hero. One exists inside of you right now. Give yourself power and responsibility to rise to the occasion. You have the right to stand up for yourself and bring order to your own life. The only superpower you need is a small bit of courage. You can take the first step and practice moving forward towards the direction you want to go.

263. Feeling happy is not being happy. It is possible to use medications to produce chemical reactions that would cause of a variety of positive feelings, but that is not to be confused with actually being happy. Happiness generally is the result of a lifestyle of healthy choices and is often built over time. You have the ability to make daily changes by starting small and working towards improving your whole life so that you may experience happiness more often.

264. Replace time goals with actions you have control over. An easy way to reduce stress is to alter how you view when you expect to be some place. You may schedule leaving your house by a specific time, but a lot can happen from the time when you wake up and the time you walk out the door. Instead, make a list of actions you want to complete before leaving and set a time for when you start that procedure. Just remember to give yourself a few extra minutes of grace time so that if something does come up, you will not feel rushed.

265. You can ask that others let go of details. Many times in a conversation, you may be expected to provide specific information. One easy thing to ask from others is to request they help by giving you some slack on providing those details. While learning to live with a mental illness, making an effort to recount such details is probably difficult and to be asked to so may only add lots of stress.

266. You can make your life story more positive. Perhaps you feel that your past is mostly negative or that your memories are more like nightmares. Try focusing on what you can do today to begin to create more positive events in your life. Start small and in time, you will begin to have new memories to reflect upon.

267. You may not be the first to notice improvements in your condition. While recovering from clinical depression, it may be the case that you are not the first to see improvements. Other people in your life, especially those closest to you may notice changes before you do. Do not get discouraged by this. For many, this is how recovery happens and it is a good sign that you are getting healthier.

268. A good friend tells the real truth. Be wary of anyone that attempts to justify telling you that clinical depression is a condition that just goes away on its own. People often mean well, but may give advice based on limited or false information. Severe medical conditions do not just simply vanish. Illnesses stay with you unless there is intervention. A good friend will be realistic and encouraging. He or she will help you get the assistance you need and encourage you to make the changes necessary to improve your health.

269. Positive thinking alone most certainly will not cure you. There are many wonderful aspects to thinking positively about situations. However, clinical depression, like all physical ailments, requires more than just a change in thinking to stop its progression. Consult specialists, make lifestyle changes, and give yourself time to heal.

270. Yes, language is sometimes limiting. It is hard to communicate what life is like while suffering from a severe medical condition and it is even more difficult for you when the condition shares its name with a common emotion. You are not going crazy and most find it frustrating to talk to others. You may consider taking the time to describe your depression as a medical condition and that it is not an emotion, but an actual physical aliment.

271. It is okay if you are scared. Sometimes really scary things happen to you, so being fearful is a good sign. Being healthy means a lot more than just feeling well, it also means you react emotionally to life events in a way that makes sense to you. If something scary is happening, it most certainly makes sense that you are scared.

272. Carefully explain yourself to medical professionals so you are understood. You will likely find that it is a good use of your energy to take the time to thoroughly explain the origins of your thoughts. It is important to doctors and therapists what observations you have that originate out of your obsessions, dreams, or reality. You may also find it easier to clarify exactly how you are suffering if you can describe your thoughts as unwelcome, invasive, or just passive. A few descriptive words can go a long way to communicating efficiently.

273. Do not dismiss a less experienced medical professional. Sometimes a doctor that is new to the practice can provide insights that an expert doctor may not have thought of. A therapist new to the profession may have more experience with ideas that were recently proven through research. You can give a professional new to the medical field a chance to help you, especially if you feel a new approach might be helpful.

274. Try being thankful for something different. Today, select something new to appreciate. Stop and take a minute to acknowledge something in the world that you are grateful of that perhaps you have not noticed in a while. It may help alter your perspective of your reality, even if just for a short while.

275. Happiness is the result many of your actions. One single life change probably will not bring more happiness into your life, but making several changes might. Happiness is also more than a frame of mind or collection of positive thoughts. Thinking more positively can go a long way to relieving much suffering, but you will find that your actions also play a huge role in the quality of your life.

276. Sometimes staying busy is best. There may be times while you are ill when the best way to cope is just to stay busy. Consider keeping your hands in motion by doing something safe and productive like folding clothes or doing a few push-ups. You might also try being creative and make a piece of art. Maybe you just need to do something repetitive like organizing your pantry or alphabetizing your books or movies. Some nights might be rough, so maybe you just need to allow your mind to do something very boring and dull for a few hours. It is okay. Some nights, staying safe will have to be your top priority, so do not worry about small stuff like how weird what you have to do might be. Some nights, you just need to play with watercolors all night or do several word search puzzles. It is fine.

277. Unplug for an hour. Turn off all electronics and refrain from using them for an hour or even a whole day. Assess how you feel afterwards. You may find that being connected to so much technology is actually adding to your stress, anxiety, or clinical depression. Try unplugging an hour before going to bed or while you are working on important projects. You might find it easier to accomplish self-care type tasks when you are not plugged into so much technology.

278. Take some time to unclutter your space. Extra stuff can add extra stress to your life. Consider owning fewer items. If the task of discarding things is too hard right now, try reorganizing the ones you have. Try relocating five items to better fit your needs. If that works well, then try five more. In time, you can work towards a full assessment of your stuff. You may feel less anxious once you develop a method of discarding items that no longer serve you any purpose.

279. Let go of the idea of perfectionism. You might yearn for something to work perfectly or be perfect, but it most likely is not the best of ideals to hold on to. Each time something in your life does not meet your high expectation of perfection, the disappointment probably adds stress to your life. Consider rethinking how you view your job, your projects, your beliefs, your relationships, and even yourself. Shift the focus from perfect to just healthy and ask if your job, project, belief, relationship, or self-image is healthy for you.

280. Prepare for the future by thinking ahead. There is no need to obsess about what may happen tomorrow, but if you have the energy, taking a few moments to prepare can greatly reduce your stress level tomorrow. Lay out the clothes you want to wear, double check your to-do list or calendar, and mentally walk through all the important things that you want to happen. Taking just a few moments to plan may greatly reduce your anxiety, just do not get carried away and start obsessing. You might lose track of time and you deserve to make the most of this day too.

281. Crying is a part of the human experience. Try not to hold back tears. When you can and feel safe to do so, allow yourself to cry. Even if you are too depressed to feel relief right now, a little bit of crying might help you feel less stressed.

282. Take the time to say good-bye. Making the decision to let something go may be very good for you, but so is taking the time to say a proper good-bye. It is important to acknowledge all the time and energy you spent on something, even if it will no longer help you in the way you need in the future. It is okay to say a proper good-bye to something, a person, or an idea. Your life, all parts of it, deserves that kind of validation by you.

283. You are not a flawed and defective person. What is happening to you right now is not your whole identity. Your experiences may be unfortunate. Situations may be unfavorable.

Plans of actions that you design may have flaws. A car you drive may have parts that are defective, but not you. You are a person with an identity that is unique and special. That identity is not flawed or defective. Keep your identity out of the mix when you pinpoint areas of your life you wish to improve.

284. You are whole and complete. It may not feel that way right now, but you are a complete person worthy of love and kindness. You may feel that you need something else, something in addition to yourself to be complete, but you do not. You do not need something outside of yourself in order to be fully human, real, and your honest self.

285. Practice establishing self-worth from the inside out. You may feel that with so many medical professionals working with you that your progress can only be measured through their perspective. Over time, you may also begin to feel that your value is determined by them too. It is not. You have the power to understand that you have intrinsic worth. Practice every day standing up for that ability and try your best to not let any medical diagnosis and its treatment take that from you.

286. Make an effort to be more vulnerable. You may find an urge to control as much as you can as often as you can. Let some of the need to control things go. Allow a little bit of vulnerability into your life. In time, by letting go of a small amount of control, you will learn to trust again.

287. Your needs are okay. You may feel that since some of your needs are different they are wrong or unworthy of your energy to protect them. In truth, your honest self is worthy of your compassion, loyalty, and kindness. Practice every day believing that all your needs are valid and worthy.

288. Identify, prioritize, plan, and take action. This is a cycle of thinking you can practice to provide yourself some relief. Identifying a problem that is within your control and ability to fix is the first step. Then, prioritize which parts of the problem need to be addressed first. Make a list or plan of action remembering to keep steps very small. Act on your plan and reward yourself for all of your victories. You may discover a different healthy method that works better for you, and that is fine.

289. A little guilt is okay. Sometimes you feel guilty because you committed an act that went against your beliefs. You might feel some guilt, which will encourage you to make amends with that wrongdoing and move on with your life. When your guilt is so massive that you stop treating yourself with respect and kindness, then that is less okay.

290. Try relaxing your emotions. You may find that exercises in relaxing your physical body do not provide enough relief for you. Think about trying exercises to relax your emotions too. Remove yourself from emotional triggers. Attempt a healthy emotional release like laughter, crying, or talking. You might aim to take some time to do something quiet that you find peaceful. You may think of other healthy ways to give your emotions a break, which is fine too.

291. Not all times of the day are equal. You may feel that some parts of the day are more stressful than others. You are not going crazy, it is normal to experience stress in this fashion. Spend a few days trying to identify a pattern. You may be surprised what parts of your day are giving you the most hardship. Give yourself extra attention when you know your stress level probably will increase and practice healthy coping skills. Reflect on the possibility of making more permanent changes to decrease your stress level.

292. Anger is not a bad emotion. There are good reasons for anger to exist. Part of your human experience involves experiencing this emotion on some level some of the time. However, there are levels of anger that are unhealthy, but that does not make it wrong or bad.

293. You can say no. Practice saying no to someone when you are asked to do something you do not feel comfortable doing or would otherwise rob you of your energy. You deserve to use your energy to propel your recovery forward towards a healthier future. It is okay to say no.

294. Examine consequences. You may find that you are not sure what the next step may be. One way to determine your actions is to consider each of their possible results. While you cannot predict the future with certainty, you may find that after thinking about the cause and effect relationship of events to the end, one may emerge as a wiser choice.

295. Try expressing yourself more. Every day find a way to express what you are experiencing and feeling. There are many different ways to do this, but common ways include writing, working on an art project, or building something.

296. There is more than one way to get your needs met. You are capable and creative enough to invent new ways to accomplish meeting your needs. You have the power to try alternative methods of satisfying them without resorting to unhealthy means to do so. It may take time and energy, but you deserve it.

297. Treat yourself. There is no need to wait for someone else to give you a nice present. Give yourself flowers, a new outfit, or a night out. You deserve the occasional indulgence, just stay within your budget and make sure it will take away stress, not add to it.

298. Learn something new today. Put forth the energy, concentration, and effort to learn something brand new. You may find that focusing on the task is rewarding and pleasing. New knowledge is often a good thing and it strengthens the mind.

299. Do not stress about following plans exactly. Sometimes you try very hard to follow all the details of your plan, but still something unexpected happens. That is okay. Try your best to do what you can when you are able. Make peace with knowing you are doing your best.

300. Ask yourself what are the most important things that you want out of life. The answer, once you really stop and think about it, might surprise you. Devote a few minutes to trying to connect with and identify the most important things that you want. Focus on what you your current life needs right now before looking into your possible future.

301. Cut yourself off from what drains you. You deserve relationships and commitments that bring you energy. If a friendship is more draining than helpful, perhaps it is time to move on. If your hobby or social event is taking more from you than you are getting back, then it might be time to try new activities.

302. Avoid scary movies and lots of drama. Your real, current life likely has enough pain and suffering for you to worry about right now. Try selecting a good comedy when you yearn for a nice story and leave the fictional emotional roller coasters alone for a while.

303. The world is not ending, it just might seem that way. Tomorrow, this beautiful lovely planet Earth is still going to be here. You lack the ability to destroy it. You really do not have a personal relationship with Earth's future. Nothing you can say or do is going to cause the world to self-destruct. Go ahead and live your life and understand it is okay if you make mistakes. Your mistakes will not irreversibly harm the universe. You have a lot of power, but not *that* kind of power.

304. Sometimes you have to be your own knight in shining armor. It is okay to be your own savior, victor, or bringer of all that is good and wonderful. You can create a healthier life without waiting for anyone's permission. All you need to start moving forward is your own commitment to the goal of positive change.

305. Choose to be more powerful. What you take from any given situation will give you more power to create the life you want or remove some power from you. The responsibility lies in you to make that choice every single day.

306. Letting go does not mean pretending it did not happen. It just simply means you are releasing all of that draining stress and emotions to make room for more positive stuff. It is recognizing that you deserve to live today in the fullest, free of all weighed emotional baggage.

307. You must accept reality, but you do not have to approve it.
Reality has existed and will continue to exist as its own entity. It will
not wait for your permission to press on forward. Your unique
perception of reality is simply the version you were given, which
you also do not need to feel pressure to approve of either. You can
release yourself from that burden.

308. Figure out in which environment you do your best. You may
need to listen to music, expose yourself to more sunlight, or warm
yourself up a bit by putting on a sweater. If you have the ability, you
may put up new pictures, paint a room a different color, or rearrange
furniture. Discovering what you need in your environment to do
your best work may lift your mood and provide you with more
energy.

309. List everything you can think of that is bothering you. Write
it or type it, it does not matter, but attempt to take an inventory of all
the things that seem wrong to you. Afterwards, review your list and
see if a pattern emerges. You may find that many of the things that
bother you stem from one major stressor or originate from the same
environment. Even if no pattern emerges, it may just be helpful and
reduce your stress to get everything written down.

310. You do not have to build a life around what you are good at.
What you like to do and what you are naturally talented at doing
may be very different and that is okay. You are not obligated to
pursue your natural talents. Instead, think about building your life
around your passions. This shift may add more meaning and purpose
to your life as you work towards goals that truly excite you.

311. You probably will not receive praise from others and that is okay. You do not need to wait around for other people in your life to give you credit for a job well done. You know when you are giving it your all and when things go well. Choose to give yourself praise when you deserve it and as often as you want.

312. Refrain from dumping your feelings onto others. You do not have the right to bundle up your negative emotions and throw them at other humans. Instead, find healthier channels to release negative energy. Try taking a walk, building something, listening to music, or practicing calming breathing exercises. You do have control over when you choose to rework all of that negativity out of your body, so choose to stay kind to others.

313. Give yourself rewards for effort. Focusing on progress and accomplishments is fun, but remember to give yourself credit and rewards for all of your effort. The fact that you are dedicating a lot of your time and energy to working on recovery is also worthy of your praise.

314. Treat your body with respect. Your body is beautiful and wonderful. At times while coping with a mental illness, it may seem ugly or broken, but it is not. Now more than ever, your body needs your attention and care. Be gentle to your physical self and treat it with kindness.

315. Wait a day before making big purchases. You never need to feel obligated to promise a lot of your money towards any kind of purchase without taking the time to really think it over. You deserve to see your money go to where it will serve you the most. Take the time to consider if your purchase will help you move forward towards a healthier future.

316. Select positive or happy passwords for your accounts. You may enter passwords several times during the day or week. Choose to make them remind you of something pleasant, so that every time you type one in, you will recall for a moment a feeling of joy.

317. Try a new recipe. Foods might taste different to you than they did before, but try new foods anyway. Your first attempt at the new meal might not turn out well, but keep trying. In time, you may find new healthier meals that are less stressful to prepare.

318. Refrain from making changes just for the sake of changing things. Some things need to stay the same because they are working well for you. Only change routines, habits, lifestyle choices, and relationships when the change is needed. Avoid making changes in an effort to strive for perfection or to put your mark on something. Have your mark be the wisdom to leave something alone when it is serving its purpose.

319. Wear clothes that fit you well. You are the only one that knows which size is printed on your clothing label. Ignore the small detail of that number or letter and focus on if it fits you appropriately. Wear clothes that are comfortable so that you can focus your thoughts on other matters.

320. Only you can move yourself towards an opportunity. Others may provide an opportunity for you, but it is your choice and your actions that will help you succeed. Try not to wait too long to take advantage of it. Ask for help if you need it, but remember, it will be you that takes the first steps and sees it through to the end.

321. If you want something different, you will have to do things differently. It may feel comfortable and safe to do the same things repeatedly, but only by taking the initiative to do something new will you likely experience growth. Rare events may happen that might alter the course of your life, but for full recovery and progress towards a healthier you, the events that happen will most likely originate from your actions.

322. Choose actions that reflect your values. It is okay to have faith and beliefs. Your priorities are truly yours. Your values are for you to decide. However, having values and living your life by them are two different things entirely. Making decisions and acting in accordance with your values is most likely how you will achieve a purposeful life.

323. Select your actions based on your priorities. It is one thing to make a goal and a list of smaller subgoals to help achieve it. However, your first real test will probably be taking action based on your decision to make something a priority in the first place. The small decisions you make each day impact your future. Choose to commit to the goals you value by making choices that move you towards what you believe to be most important.

324. Replace any thoughts of needing to be perfect. You need not focus on obtaining perfection, just focus on being real. Real people have moments of excellence and periods of dullness. Real people have feelings, desires, and occasionally make mistakes. Real people, like you, can work for a better future. You deserve a real life filled with real happiness, so focus on being a real person.

325. Think more about the benefits of work, not how hard you work. The actual details of hard work can rob you of your desire to even get started. It is okay to think about the outcome and benefits of your work. It is fine to take a minute to imagine standing at the finish line before you start. You may feel more motivated and excited to devote the effort if you take a moment to remind yourself why you want to work at something.

326. You have limits, but over time they too may change. The kinds of things that are holding you back now will probably be different in the future. Assuming a goal that is not possible today will also be impossible in the future may be unrealistic. The future version of you might be able to handle your goal just fine.

327. Visualize the process of living a life free from symptoms of depression. Spend some time imaging what it would be like to live a healthy day free from all your aliments. Focus on the process of living that day. Think of all the details, the routines, the order in which you would carry out tasks. Imagine the specific actions you would choose. Consider choosing to do some of those actions today. You might discover a new method of reaching some of your goals.

328. Do something you know is good for you. It may be hard to carry out a healthy task when it does not feel good to do so, but do it anyway. Continue to treat yourself to your good deeds regardless of the fact those deeds do not feel the same as they once did. The severe medical condition that is depression may have temporary robbed your body of its ability to enjoy your good efforts, but go ahead and spoil yourself. In time, it most likely will start to feel good again.

329. Keep a busy list. Brainstorm a simple list of activities you can do the next time you encounter some downtime. Tuck a short list into your planner or purse. Consider making a list of things to do with company too. Free time is less scary if you have a plan of action already thought out ahead of time to turn to for ideas.

330. Create a daily basic self-care schedule. As the severe medical condition that is depression worsens, the need for your own self-care schedule will become increasingly necessary. Try to include eating, bathing, getting dressed, and other tasks that are necessary for your own care. The great benefit to this schedule is how useful it will continue to be throughout your treatment and recovery. You may love it so much that you keep one for years to come because it frees your decision making skills to focus on other activities.

331. Change your goals when you do not see progress. It is okay to let go of goals, at least temporarily, when you are not seeing any kind of progress. You can always return to the same goal later. Work towards a different goal for a while. You deserve to see positive results of your actions and making a goal change might be the healthiest thing you can do right now.

332. Try not to obsess over avoiding negativity or failure. Bad stuff will still happen sometimes even when you work very hard and put forth a lot of effort. You are working hard to improve your overall quality of life. That means it is okay if something bad happens occasionally. A small set back does not mean you have failed or are flawed.

333. You can be specific about your feelings. You may be tempted to simplify your emotional pain by using vague vocabulary. There are different kinds of pain and sadness. There are many words to describe each emotion. Try being detailed and specific about how you honestly feel. There are differences between pain, sadness, numbness, and apathy. Choosing to be more descriptive helps you communicate more efficiently.

334. Educate yourself about your medical condition. Knowledge may really be power in this case, but it is possible to overdo it. Learn what you can so that you know enough to separate out your identity from the illness. You deserve to retain your sense of self throughout your recovery process.

335. You are able to be selective about your worries. Just as you might prioritize your goals and dreams, consider prioritizing your worries. There is no need to worry about everything anyway, so just focus on a selective few that really bother you. Focus on defining them and how to resolve your anxiety and fear.

336. Refrain from tolerating items that are not working well. You have enough to keep track of and be responsible for right now. You do not need to deal with items in your home that are not working properly. Invest in properly functioning alarm clocks, appliances, and other items that you use daily. You deserve to live in a less stressful environment. All of those small inconveniences add up to be a major stressor.

337. Be prepared for reasonable events. There are things you can prepare for without obsessing about their consequences. Keeping an umbrella in your car or purse is not a sign of paranoia but of appropriate precaution. Taking a book with you when you run errands is a sign of smart planning since often you may find yourself waiting in a long line. There are simple things you can do to plan ahead that are smart, sensible, and will reduce anxiety or worry.

338. Give compliments often. Say nice things to others and to yourself. Praise things and decisions you like or find enjoyable. If you admire your friend's choice in shoes, say so. If you are impressed with your neighbor's garden, tell him. You do not need to wait for an invitation to share your admiration.

339. You can work smarter, without working harder. There is a limit to the amount of energy you can devote to your life. Refrain from putting yourself down because you cannot do more. Instead, refocus your energy more intelligently by shifting your attention to what you believe is the most important use of your time.

340. Eat for energy, not for your emotions. Try to refrain from using food as a reward or motivation. Food is a necessary part of life so respect it as such. Strive to eat foods that give you energy and are filling. You deserve to enjoy your meals without worry. Making a commitment to view food as simply just a necessity may prevent you from trying to turn food into something more than it is.

341. Finding new friends is about finding new places. If you continue with the same routines, you will keep running into the same people. Check out an events calendar, research other areas in your community, and seek out activities that interest you. At first, you might possibly be going alone, but in time, you will meet new people. Some may eventually become your friends.

342. Forgive a stranger. You may find that your life path crosses with people who happen to be jerks, rude, or otherwise just plain mean. Instead of allowing their actions to create further stress in your life, forgive them. After all, they are strangers and since you will not ever see them again prevent yourself from seeing their negativity again by letting go.

343. Abstain from panicking about the future. You have time to build the kind of future that you want. There is little reason to panic about it because you are capable of taking action right now, even if those actions are just mental steps, to create that high quality future you deserve.

344. Your emotions and attitude may influence each other. At times your negative attitude may control your emotions. Often, this manifests as anger. Try your best to accept responsibility for your attitude and realize that most of the time, emotions and attitude are two different things. With practice, it is possible to prevent one from immediately affecting the other.

345. Your attention is a gift. Be selective on who and what you choose to focus on and take part in. You attention is very meaningful and powerful. It is how you can show love and compassion even when you do not feel well. It is a way you can express and communicate what ideas you feel are worthy of your time and interest.

346. It is okay to be selfish on occasion. It is difficult for you to take care of others or complete responsibilities if you are not well. Occasionally you need to just say no to commitments and do something for yourself. Basic self-care is not a luxury but something you need to do so that you can stay healthy. Acts of kindness towards you are also likely a requirement for staying healthy and happy too.

347. Refrain from trying to buy happiness. There is no amount of money in the world and no magical amount of stuff that will banish the symptoms of clinical depression and fill you with happiness. That is simply not how the human experience works. Often, the way to happiness is both simpler and friendlier to your bank account. Practice healthy habits with a positive attitude. In time, happiness will find you.

348. Life is not fair, but that is not your problem to fix. The more you obsess about how unfair your current life situation is, the more it will hold you back from creating the future you want to live. The more you attempt to make life fairer for others, the less energy you have to help yourself get to the place where you need to be. Try your best to not take it all personally and move on forward towards a better future free of resentment.

349. You do not need to suffer in silence. It can be difficult to explain to others how much you are suffering, but sometimes you need to try. There are some aspects of your condition that can only be explained with words and probably only after several attempts. That is okay, keep trying to connect with people you trust. What you are going through is hard to handle alone.

350. Tomorrow may not be better, but it will be different. If today is overwhelming you, take comfort in knowing tomorrow will be different. It may not be as different as you want it to be, but you will have new opportunities, new feelings to deal with, and a new chance to make some changes. You may even have more control over what is happening. Take a deep breath, hang on, and wait for a new day.

351. Live within your financial means. Spend only what you have and refrain from overspending. Aim to only take out loans when you need to and have a plan for paying them back. Being in financial debt may add great stress to your life. Occasionally you cannot help accumulating debt, but if you can, making adjustments to your lifestyle may be a better option for you.

352. It is okay to pack up and leave. Maybe you need a completely new start. Maybe the only way to make it happen is by relocating to a different city. You are not a failure if you just need a different city to call home. Make sure to thoroughly research and set up care for yourself before relocating. If possible, try to save up enough money to live on while you get settled. Understand it may take a year or so to set up a support network with new friends. If you have the patience, moving might be the best thing for you to do.

353. You are not a statistic. You may find information about your condition and find all the information disheartening. Just because others made decisions that gave them a future that you find unsatisfactory does not mean you are destined for the same future. You can make your own future.

354. It is okay to not care. Every so often it is all you can do. There are times that you just do not care about something and that is fine. You may have whole days where nothing seems to be worthy of your interest. You are ill. It is okay to feel this way for a little while.

You are not a failure, permanently broken, or a lost cause. You are just coping today and that is alright.

355. Consider only paying for non-essentials with cash. If you are trying to spend less money on a whim, try limiting your extra spending to cash purchases only. This cuts out online purchases and most of the time prevents overspending. Twenty dollars takes on a whole new meaning and may become more valuable to you when you watch it leave your hand. It also may motivate you to leave the house more, which may be just what you need right now.

356. Make commitments to the real world. Watch less TV, spend less time on the internet, and limit your social media usage. You can redirect your attention to something in the room with you right now, something you can interact with, something you can experience. Focusing on the real environment around you may help you become more self-aware of your state of being. The more you know about your current self, the easier it probably is to identify what you need to do in order help it feel better. Be kind to yourself by showing up in the present, in the real world and make you the priority it deserves to be.

357. Activities are probably a lot less interesting, but do them anyway. Clinical depression may have robbed you of the joy you used to feel when you participated in activities. You may feel discouraged or frustrated, but continue to live your life. Try completing the tasks that brought you fulfillment in the past. In time, you will begin to feel pleasure again. Practice putting you first, even when it does not feel good.

358. Stop seeking out people who want to be with the depressed you. Seek out people that want to be around a healthy you and will be supportive of your efforts to recover. Seek out people who care enough to listen, but will remind you repeatedly that you are capable of more. Spend your time working towards forming a healthy social network of people who will pick you up, not push you down further. You deserve positive influences, not more reinforcements of the ill-mannered self-talk possibly happening in your mind right now.

359. You are not lazy. You are a person, not a single word adjective. You may have moments when you feel lazy or choose to not do something. You probably have good reason for choosing inaction, so take responsibility for your lack of action and call it elective idleness. If your symptoms are severe enough that you are in state of lethargic misery, then it is outside of your control. Either way, you are not lazy, you are just a human trying to make it through another day, so avoid belittling yourself down to a lone descriptive word. You are much more than that.

360. Suicidal thinking is sign you are not well, not a selfish attempt to get attention. In order to pursue something in your self-interest, you would first need to understand what would interest you or bring you pleasure. Clinical depression generally does an efficient job of robbing you of your ability to feel joy or pleasure from any actions, even extreme ones such as thoughts of suicide. The idea that your self-destructive behavior is selfish is highly illogical since odds are that you gain nothing from the behavior that pleases you. Try your best to refrain from assuming that your desire to request help when you are feeing suicidal is somehow a shameful act of attention seeking. It is not. You need help so take appropriate action immediately. You deserve to receive adequate medical attention when you are this severely unwell. Doing so makes you responsible, not selfish.

361. Step outside of your comfort zone, but think small. There is no need to sprint away from what makes you comfortable. However, in order to make the kinds of changes you may need in order to progress towards the kind of future you want, some movement by you is required. If something scares you, take small steps to overcome your fear. If something causes great anxiety, then consider small exercises to begin to overcome it. In time, you can expand your comfort zone to include the environments and tasks you need to achieve the kind of life you desire.

362. Give an hour of your time. Your time is a gift. Choose to dedicate an hour of it to another person. Help a neighbor mow her lawn, listen to a family member tell a story, assist a friend with a move, or spend an hour volunteering in your community. You most likely will find some sense of purpose in helping others and it may help take your thoughts off your struggles for a short while.

363. Understand there will always be things that are unknown. No person knows everything, nor does any philosophy or religion. You are allowed to react to the unknown any way you want. You can pray more, read more, think more, or ignore it all. It is up to you to decide how much value you want to place on what is unknown to you. You have the right and power to do so.

364. Have a date with your money. Make a nice meal, put on fancy clothes, and get comfortable. Spend the evening with your budget. Sit down, listen to soothing music, and go over your spending and savings. You can research ways to spend money more wisely, make lists about how you want to invest in your future, or even just cut coupons for your next grocery store trip. Reviewing your finances does not have to be a negative emotional experience.

365. Hold onto something safe. With clinical depression, there may be times when the symptoms are painful and seem overwhelming. Grab something that is not harmful, something you cannot use to hurt yourself, and hold onto it. Lay down with it, attempt to sleep with it still in your hands, and do not let go. It may sound a bit silly, but it also may be very effective to get you through the worst of your struggles.

366. From time to time getting angry is good for you. As long as you take the energy that feeds your anger and channel it into something positive and productive, anger may occasionally serve you well. Anger is possibly not the healthiest emotion, but there are some experiences you may have that make you justifiably angry. In such cases, turn that anger into a type of passion and use it to do some good in the world. Some of the best non-profits, success stories, and art projects have been born from this kind of passion.

367. It probably is a good idea for you to have a back-up plan. You are going to change and your priorities may change with you. When creating a vision for your future, create alternative journeys that may lead you to the same destination and also other endpoints with which you feel you may be equally satisfied. Being a little bit flexible on the details will likely relieve you of stress and anxiety too, which is also a good thing.

368. Set a reminder alarm to start your bedtime routine. It is easy to get caught up in evening activities or distracted by unforeseen events. By creating some kind of reminder alarm, you are training yourself to take your bedtime routine and your night's sleep a whole lot more seriously. Working towards a healthy sleep schedule will probably greatly benefit your overall health, especially your symptoms of depression.

369. Never stop learning about you, your life, and the world around you. Allow your perceptions and understandings to be changed by knowledge and experience. You deserve an enlightened human experience. Continuing to learn might result in the discovery of new hobbies, interests, and in time, more friends.

370. Write a letter to a former you. Take the time to sit down and give a past you advice. Even if you choose to write it to a version of you that existed a few days ago, you may find this exercise greatly beneficial. It will give you an opportunity to identify and write down what you have learned since then, which may help you realize that your current situation is not as hopeless as you first thought. You have learned a lot since the beginning of your journey. Give yourself credit for that.

371. Try not to snooze in the morning. It is very hard to avoid, but if possible, do not hit snooze. You may find it easier to cope with you symptoms if you wake up at the same time each day and allow for naps. Just try not to nap too late in the day because that may disrupt your bedtime routine.

372. It is possible to take it all too seriously. Learning to live with or overcome a serious medical condition is a very big and very real thing. However, it is possible to just put too much pressure on yourself to turn your experiences into something explainable, justifiable, and plausible. Occasionally, what you are going through is just so ridiculous that it is actually a little humorous. It is okay to laugh at it all sometimes.

373. You have the right to find zero purpose in your suffering. You can choose to write it off as a no good, very bad time and continue on the same life path you had before you got ill. Not everything you experience in life has to be soul changing. There is no reason to feel guilty for not being more influenced by your situation. Sometimes there is no point, cause, or lesson that you feel worthy to take from a life experience and it is your right to form that opinion.

374. You are more than a body. Your physical appearance and existence is just a part of who you are. You have many other aspects that identify you. Your value cannot be captured in a simple photograph or weighed on a simple scale. You are more than a number, more than a size, more than an oxygen-consuming being, and more than you may have ever realized.

375. Avoid triggers, even small ones. You will probably figure out what kinds of things impact your moods in a very negative way. These triggers may not all be avoidable, but when they are it is your responsibility to stay clear of them. Choose to make it a priority to limit exposure to these triggers.

376. Find courage to let go of the things you cannot change or control. There will always be some stuff that is not within your control or power to alter. It takes life experience to know what you actually have control over, but it takes courage to make the steps necessary to change them.

377. Try making a list of what you do not want. Occasionally answering the question of what you want or desire is in itself overwhelming. Consider instead describing or listing what you do not want out of life or your future. It is a starting place and your list may be long, but it is still important. Use this to help you brainstorm other kinds of futures you may enjoy living.

378. There may be people you encounter who just will never understand. Stop wasting your time and energy explaining things to them. It is not your duty to drag others out of their ignorance. You may find it useful to share resources with them, but stop short of taking on the responsibility of their enlightenment. That is their journey in their life and certainly not your top problem right now.

379. You may have to temporarily settle and that is okay. You may have to take a job that is not exactly in your field of interest, you may have to live in a neighborhood that is not located in the best spot for you, or you may have to finish completing an education that you wish you could just avoid entirely. Sometimes you are on a life path that needs to happen, but it is a temporary stopping point for you to reestablish your goals and priorities. You have not failed and you are not stuck. Take pride in the income earned, the safe home you create, and the new knowledge you acquire. When you can, take the next step.

380. Keep a morning snack at your bed side to help with morning energy. It may be difficult to get up and walk to your kitchen when you first wake up and that is okay. Just keep a snack and maybe a bottle of water or juice next your bed so you can reach over and grab it first thing. Refrain from keep a supply of food next to your bed. Perhaps make this snack a nutritious but not necessarily a yummy one. You still want to try to get up out of bed and eat regular meals.

381. Start imagining what life would be like if everything went right. Consider what it is that you actually want to have happen to you and spend some time daydreaming about it. You may want to even write it all down. You may find it empowering to see your future in this positive way, even if it is for the moment a figment of your imagination.

382. Try counting to twenty or counting even numbers to a hundred. A quick way to decrease anxiety may be to refocus your thoughts on a counting task. After a few rounds reciting what suits your mood at the moment, try slowing down and breathing deeply between numbers. It may not solve your underlining problem, but it may help you regain enough control of your body to shift over to more long-lasting coping strategies to hold you over until it either passes or you can get medical care.

383. Take everything slow. You are fighting a battle with a severe medical condition that is very difficult to live with. Try to do each task you do very slowly. Take frequent breaks and understand that there will be bad days when you take a long time to get anything done. That is okay. It does not necessarily mean you are getting more ill, it may just not be a good day for you and that is fine.

384. It is difficult to relax and panic at same time. Your body can only do so much at once, so if you feel your body becomes extremely stressed, anxious, or worried, try a relaxation exercise. Many people, including most medical professionals, are open to sharing relaxation tips and exercises so this would be a great thing to ask others to assist you in discovering. Slow, deep breathing is always a good exercise to try first.

385. If you do not know what you want to do, just do something new and different. Every so often the world before you may seem vast and endless. If you do not know what will make you happy or bring you a step closer to a healthier future, then consider just doing something very different. As long as it is legal, is not harmful, or otherwise a hardship, trying something new may help you understand yourself more and discover what might make you happy in the future.

386. Let your heart, mind, and soul guide you on your path to a better life. Sometimes the right thing for you to do is politically incorrect, goes against the social standard, and is questionably reckless. The truth is that what you define as right for you will always be right, no matter where the current culture stands on the issue.

387. Be a lot nicer to the world at large, especially to yourself. It may take more effort if your symptoms of clinical depression are bothersome, but in the long run being nice is probably best. When you think about how you talk to and treat yourself, make sure it is with kindness even when it is hard to do. You spend more time with you than anyone else so it is important that you treat yourself with compassion.

388. Occasionally, it really is the weather that is affecting your emotions and happiness. You are not crazy. Moods are effected by a lot more in your environment than you are able to control so do not be too hard on yourself. Practice healthy habits of coping and wait it out. New weather will appear soon.

389. Life may not provide an obvious right choice. Ideally, we want our array of choices to include one that is obviously fantastic. However, often this is not the case. Occasionally we will have to select between an option that is bad and one that is even worse. Do the best with what you are given and choose the best option available. It is the most you realistically can do, so be at peace with that.

390. No one is out to get you. There is no conspiracy to hurt you. There may be a greedy drug company, a doctor who is unprofessional, or a therapist who is not teaching you the best coping strategies. However, there is no grand conspiracy to hold you back or hurt you. Most drug companies are truly trying to produce medicines that help you get better. Most doctors truly want to see you get well. Most therapists take the time to teach you the most valuable skills you need to know. Encountering one bad person or organization does not mean the rest of the planet is trying to inflict pain upon you. It just means you need to be proactive and seek out new help.

391. Take ownership of your actions. You may need or want to do something, which is fine. Call your actions what they are, your actions. They are a reflection of your needs and your wants, no one else's. You are under no obligation to do things for others. If you do, it is because you wanted to, so accept that.

392. New hobbies can start out as small tasks. If the idea of a hobby seems overwhelming, then focus on something small. Try drawing, origami, or crafting a poem. Don't obsess about keeping it or storing it. Just focus on exploring your creativity for a few moments. You may find it peaceful and relaxing to take a few seconds and produce something original.

393. There is no universal method of recovery. There is no single right way to recover from depression. It is okay if something you attempt does not work for you. It is okay to give something a try and for it to fail. It does not mean your clinical depression is not treatable. It just means you have learned that something does not work for you, so try something else. It may take several attempts before you find something that works well. Try your best to be patient and understanding. You can continue to treat yourself with compassion.

394. For short periods of time, you may have to work with the pain. Yes, it my be painful to get out of bed, put on clothes, and transport yourself to a doctor or therapist appointment, but you need to do this anyway. You may be in so much pain that you are in tears when you show up, but try anyway. Go as far as you can, if it is too much, return home knowing that you gave it your best shot. Give yourself credit for this. Next time, push yourself a little bit farther. It will get easier.

395. Sometimes you need to change your doctor or therapist. If you feel that you cannot connect with your therapist or that your doctor is not providing you with the care you need, then seek out new help. It is okay to change doctors and switch therapists. The most important thing is to regularly visit with a licensed medical professional and to continue with your treatment plan under proper guidance.

396. Clinical depression is not personal. Depression is not a living thing that looked you up, hunted you down, and targeted you. You are simply unwell right now. For you to attempt to answer the question of why will only hold you back and slow down your healing process. Do your best to accept that this mental illness is not a sign of anything more than the fact that you are unwell.

397. You will learn a lot over the course of your treatment. Do not feel guilty about knowing something now that you did not in the beginning. You cannot go back in time and tell a previous version of yourself the new information. It is best to promise yourself that you will use the new information in the future. As you learn more about your situation, you will get better at taking care of yourself.

398. You can disagree with an idea without disliking its creator. Sometimes you may really dislike a thought, opinion, or idea and that is okay. You can say so. You can tell your friend, doctor, loved one, or stranger that their idea is not great and still believe the person is a good person. Try not to intertwine a person's worth with their actions. Every person has value that is independent of their behavior, including you.

399. Try to do the same thing differently. Consider following your previous passions, but in a different way. Try watching sporting games on the television instead of going to them. Try knitting with a different kind of yarn or shift from painting with acrylics to watercolors. There are countless ways to modify your existing interests to experiment and see if there is a better way for you to experience them.

400. Your past emotions do not shape your future happiness.
You are not destined to a future with a limited selection of moods as
determined by a severe medical condition. Allow your future to exist
as the unwritten entity that it is without any assumptions imposed
onto it before it has a chance to make an appearance.

401. You are not a ticking time bomb. The idea that once you have
been diagnosed with a mental illness that you must be mentally ill
for the rest of your life is a dramatized version of reality. It is not
healthy to wake up every day with the fear that at any moment you
will have a bad episode. You are capable of making decisions and
working towards progress every day. You can choose to focus on the
present day and your current goals. Write your own future, one
moment at a time.

402. You are equal to all others. You are not more important than
any other person, nor are you any less important. On some basic
level you are of equal worth to your worst enemy and your greatest
hero. You may have different experiences and beliefs, but you are
still equally important.

403. Make reasonable time commits to your projects. When
possible, schedule and strive for giving your work your full attention
for one hour intervals. In time, you most likely can extend that to
ninety minute intervals. After that, take a short break before
resuming your efforts. Just closing your eyes and thinking about
something else for a minute might suffice, so there may be no need
to get fancy or stressed if it is hard to get up and walk around. If it is
hard for you to pay attention for a whole hour right now, no worries.
It is just a goal to work towards. Give yourself time to work towards
developing this skill and habit.

404. Refrain from throwing money at problems. Spending money on improving your state of health or quality of life is usually a good way to use currency. However, spending money on stuff that will just add stress to your life is less healthy. Paying for expensive fees to groups, fitness centers, exclusive memberships, and classes that you lack the time or energy to take advantage of will probably not help in your recovery.

405. Noticeable comparisons may be a good sign. The ability to notice that currently you may feel worse than yesterday is actually very promising. Your observation implies you are able to notice changes happening within you on an emotional level. You have solid evidence that you are currently in a state of flux. This means that you may acknowledge your moods today as existing in a temporary state and be hopeful for a better tomorrow.

406. Practice being a clear communicator. While suffering from a severe illness, your ability to describe your symptoms accurately might be difficult. Take time before you meet with medical professionals to go over how you are going to explain your concerns. Concise and accurate self-reports will likely aid those helping you.

407. You deserve to be loved. You can choose to love yourself. There is no need to wait. You are capable of treating yourself with compassion, kindness, and admiration. You do not need permission or approval from anyone to start showing yourself kindheartedness.

408. When you hold onto anger, the only person you hurt is yourself. Do your best to realize that when you feel that you have been wronged, the best thing to do is let it go. That does not mean forgetting. It means allowing negative emotions to run their due course and let them leave. This frees you, so that you are more open to new experiences and emotions.

409. There is no need to wait for a special occasion. Wear your nice clothes, use the breakable dishes, and read that book or movie you were saving for later. You do not need to wait for a holiday or event. Today is a great day to use the good stuff and experience the luxuries you already have.

410. Devote time to your mental and emotional well-being. You may desire to improve your physical health, but also try to set aside time to take care of other aspects of yourself. Your mental health and emotional well-being also need attention from you. Practice making all different aspects of your self-care a priority.

411. Create a busy box. Consider putting together a box at your home filled with supplies to use during free time. When you experience insomnia or find that you just need to unwind but do not know what to do, you can use this box that you created to assist in passing the time.

412. Your traditions are important. Part of what defines you is customs that connect you to your own past. Practicing habits, recognizing holidays, and celebrating rituals all help create your identity. Sometimes it is not the current action that brings you meaning but the knowledge that your actions are part of a history of tradition that proves significant.

413. The tiniest stuff might bring up the biggest memories. It is okay if your memory of a past event resurfaces in full detail at the sight of something small. It can be hard to predict what things will cause you to have a strong emotional reaction. Do your best to recognize the experience as being real and valid. Consider recording your memory or acknowledging its significance in a way that is meaningful to you.

414. Accept that there exists diversity among people in the area of spiritual and philosophical ideals. You have the ability to choose among a wide variety of existing ideas, belief systems, and philosophies. Whatever area of thought or faith you select is often fine as long as it serves you well. Remember that others have the same freedom you do. Try to refrain from assumptions and judgments. Others may use their own beliefs to justify passing judgment on your medical condition, but you do not need to stoop to their level of spite.

415. Refrain from collecting or buying stuff that harms you. You deserve a safe home environment so accept responsibility for not bringing anything negative or potentially harmful into your home. Your mental and emotional safety is just as important as your physical safety. If an item causes you distress, could potentially be used for self-harm, or otherwise encourages unhealthy habits, then do not bring it into your home.

416. Success is not a road paved with perfection. A common misconception is that only perfect deeds result in excellence, but this is often not true. Your path to recovery and success will probably include a variety of events. Some you will complete efficiently, some may be spectacular failures, and some might be moments of brief misdirection. Your future is an exceptional path that you travel, embrace its uniqueness.

417. Try identifying the source of a problem in as specific manner as possible. Attempt to pinpoint the exact cause of your unsettling mood. Identifying that the cause of your sadness is a specific song you heard on the radio is much easier to deal with than declaring all music as the source of your negativity. Identifying shoes with high heels as being bothersome to your feet is much easier to work with than declaring all shoes horrible. The more precise you can be, the easier it likely will become for you to resolve your problem.

418. Some ideas only continue to exist because you keep thinking about them. There are concepts that once were useful for you that are possibly not handy anymore. If you lack any recent evidence that an idea serves you in the real world, then perhaps you should part with it. It may still be serving you in some way, but if it is not going to help you move forward towards a healthier life, then it you most likely need to let it go.

419. Your needs are valid, but so are the needs of others. When you find yourself in an argument, remember that your needs are not the only important ones. Strive to find solutions to disagreements that meet the needs of all those involved in the conflict. A good resolution will ensure that the needs of everyone are met.

420. It is okay to fail, especially when trying something for the first time. Expecting that the way to know if something is a good fit for you is that you will never fail at it is unrealistic. Failing occasionally, even at your talents and passions, is part of the human experience. Attempt to learn from your failures and keep moving in a general forward direction towards the kind of future you want to live.

421. Form opinions about the details. You might not know what will increase your happiness right now and that is okay. Focus on forming strong opinions about exactly what you do not like. When you think about your job, school, relationships, and daily life you likely will notice a few things that are extra awful. Take note of these and when an opportunity surfaces for a new job, new classes, new relationships, or a new environment consider changing to something different than what you have identified as being negative for you. After some changes, you most likely will discover something that you like more and is positive for you.

422. Clinical depression is not something you can get over, it is something you survive. It is an illness similar to conditions like pneumonia, stroke, or cancer. You developed a condition, it impacts your health, it may kill you, and you are working with medical professionals to get better. Not every one may understand this, but it is the truth of the matter. You can continue to work towards a healthier you despite misinformation that may exist. Resist the temptation to allow the ignorance of other people slow you down or impede your commitment to your recovery.

423. The things that may help the most might be the most difficult to do. You are not imagining this paradox, it exists. One of the most challenging aspects about coping with depression is learning how to resolve this awful situation. You can help yourself by admitting this is an aspect of your reality for the moment. Focus on small things you can control that will relieve some stress. In time and practice, you most likely will feel less frustrated.

424. Your comfort zone may have just shrunk to the size of a wetsuit. It is okay. Clinical depression has the ability to shrink the world you know, love, and feel comfortable living in. You can practice working towards expanding it each day by doing small tasks that are a little bit outside of your current that comfort zone. In time you can regain your original comfort zone and expand it dramatically.

425. Arrange for you to be checked up on. Part of accepting that you are ill, is accepting that you need to be looked after. Have a trusted friend or family member stop by periodically in regular, scheduled intervals to visit with you. Be open to receiving feedback about the state of your living environment and your ability to take care of yourself. While it is not your loved one's place to judge, let them observe. Listen to their feedback. It is your responsibility to accept that you need compassionate external observationto help you gage how you are doing.

426. Avoid checking out of reality. A short break into your imagination or the internet might help relieve some stress, but refrain from overdoing it. Your road to recovery will take place in your reality, not via a computer and not through a mental fantasy. It takes hard work, but you are capable of taking the first steps towards a real healthy life.

427. Your first goal probably is not recovery. The path to improved health undoubtedly contains many small goals and objectives that over a period of time may lead you to a full recovery. In the beginning, focus on reducing stress, establishing a treatment plan you understand and find purposeful. Ask lots of clarifying questions until you fully apprehend what is happening and feel like you are on the right path of progress for you.

428. Practice reacting to negative thoughts differently. You most likely will think negative thoughts throughout your life. You are human, this is one of your features. The fact that you formed a negative thought is certainly not worthy of panic. However, how you react to a negative thought may cause you great worry. It will most likely take time and persistence, but it is possible to react to your mind's creations in a healthier manner.

429. Free time is something you can make or find. There is no need to live your life waiting for free time to magically appear. You can schedule downtime and make it more of a priority. You have the freedom and power to make this happen. At first, you may only find a way to schedule a few minutes of free time each day, but you have the power to choose to make this happen.

430. There is power in giving something a name. As long as something exists in the vague world of ideas and feelings, then it may seem much bigger than it actually is. By naming something, even if it is a name that only makes sense to you, then you are taking away its power. You can start to describe it. You can start to tell its story as defined by you. You can begin to take control back and reclaim it for good.

431. Suicidal thoughts may not be a single, unusual irregularity. Potentially, at its most severe, suicidal thinking is not some kind of bizarre obsession with death. Rather, it might feel like your brain has been programed into some kind of urgent self-destruct mode. It devotes most of its time to identifying ways to terminate itself.

Commonly safe everyday objects may now be viewed by the brain as weapons. Even while sleeping, the brain may be trying to scheme of ways to terminate itself. It may not be one lone thought that is trying to dominate and conquer. It might be an army of determined thoughts persistently attempting to end you. It is important to seek out help immediately, never be left alone—not even for a few minutes, and to refrain from pushing people away. You deserve to be healthy and if enduring non-stop company is the path you need to travel for the next few days, allow it to be so.

432. Occasionally you may be the only one who understands you and that really is okay. It might be difficult to allow your own self credit and praise to be enough. However, your rationale may be the only one you can get right now. There are times in everyone's life when no one else really gets it. You are not as weird as you might think. It is okay to desire more connections with other people, but assure yourself that right now, you are providing all the validation that you truly need.

433. Avoid quickly accepting your assumptions as truth. It might be tempting to use assumptions as some kind of crutch to get you through a difficult time. However, allowing yourself to reach conclusions you formed without all the facts available is likely only generating more stressful thoughts in your head. It is stressful to go about your day making decisions and choices not based on as full an understanding of reality as possible. With every conclusion drawn from an assumption, most likely you are closing your mind off to the possibility that you need to learn more. Assumptions cannot always be avoided, so do the best you can with what is available. Just strive to make decisions based on facts as often as possible.

434. Some people are just bad for you and that is really okay.
You may encounter perfectly nice people that are unhealthy for you.
You might cross paths with someone that seems to always choose to
behave unkindly towards you. There are many reasons why a person
is just not good for you. All those reasons are okay reasons for not
letting him or her close to you. You deserve to have both healthy
relationships and people who are good for you in your life.

434. Fail better than you have ever before. Trying to avoid failure
is probably not the healthiest of habits. In your life, you will
undoubtedly try new things and most of the time you will make a
few mistakes on your way to mastering new skills. You can practice
failing better so you that get more out of each failure. When you fail,
you can focus on what you have learned, what aspects of the
situation you can improve upon next time, and reassure yourself that
you are still a great person despite something not going the way you
want the first time around.

435. People tend to remember how you make them feel. When
you encounter other people make some attempt to finish your
conversation with something positive like a saying you are thankful
for their time or shaking their hand good-bye. A simple phrase of
spoken gratitude might result in recharging the other person in the
conversation, which he or she most likely will remember feeling.
The next time you ask for some help, he or she likely will remember
that feeling and be more likely to assist you.

**436. Your life's most wonderful days probably have not
happened yet.** You may be experiencing some of the worst days of
your life. You only have the days that have already happened to you
as a comparison. Imagine the future and its possibilities. You most

likely have great days in your future, even the happiest day of your life to look forward to. Clinical depression might be creating the worst days of your life, but once the worst is over, you may only have the best days ahead of you.

437. You are so much more than who you are on any single day. What defines you is a lifetime of choices. A single day in your life most likely cannot determine every little detail about the story of your life. A single failure or accomplishment is just a small part of your identity and even then only if you let it take on such worth. You have the power to decide what you believe defines you, so choose to not allow a single day in your life predetermine your future or define your entire past.

438. Do your best to refrain from being isolated. You can find ways to be around other people in a manner that you can tolerate. Go shopping for groceries when the store is busy, greet people when you pass them on the street, go see a movie at a theater, host a small party, visit local attractions in your area, or think of other ways to be with people. There are many opportunities each day to put you near other humans, so attempt a few each day you are physically able.

439. The world as a whole has not gotten worse. Mental illness has a way of altering your perception of the reality. Despite what you may read or hear, the planet is really not going anywhere anytime soon. It is a nice, reliable home for you. The people on it are still just people. Sometimes they do horrible things, but most of the time the average person means well. There is no great misalignment with the stars that has targeted you personally. It just might feel that way sometimes, but try to take comfort in knowing the world is still here for you, because it is.

440. Consider changing the relationship you have with your problems. Really ask yourself if you have a healthy relationship with your problems. You can alter how you view difficulties and the amount of negative impact they have on your daily life. Just because something is a setback does not necessarily mean it has to add great stress and heartache. With practice, you can process your problems as just things that exist and minimize the amount of emotion you attach to them. You can choose to react in a way that allows you the ability to take charge, make changes, and continue onward.

441. Resist waiting for an invitation to take the first step. Most likely, you do not need to wait for someone else to give you permission to take action. You can do something right now to help ease your suffering that is both healthy and productive. Every so often the best course of action may be just to look for new resources or ask for help. That is always okay.

442. Set healthy boundaries between you and others. You have the ability and power to set standards for how you are treated in all of your relationships. You can also choose to enforce them by restating your expectations and removing yourself from any situation that makes you feel unsafe. If you need assistance, make sure to seek out help. You deserve to spend your time with people who are healthy for you.

443. Discontinue any comparisons you are making between yourself and others. You are living your life right now. There is very little to be gained by judging your ability to live your life well by comparing yourself to others. At most, the only comparison most find helpful is simply comparing the current you to a former you.

However, even that comparison possibly has very little benefit if you are focusing your attention on creating a healthier you for the future.

444. Sometimes you just need to take a nap and that is often okay. Every once in a while, if your current state of health can allow it, your body might need a short snooze. You may have had a restless night, perhaps nightmares disrupted your sleep, or you have worked hard and need a way to recharge. There are many ways to regain energy, but occasionally, there is no substitute for a brief nap.

445. Resist temptation to ask a person to compare you to someone else. Try not to ask a doctor how you are doing compared to other patients. Try not to ask another depressed person how you are doing compared to where they were at your stage of the condition. Try not to ask anyone to compare you to anybody. The more you simply focus on your own current self the easier it most likely will be to find the energy and courage to continue forward towards a healthier future.

446. Not all can love you the way you need to be loved. It is okay if you reach out for emotional support and the person you want to help you simply cannot. You do not have control over what a person is capable of. A person may love you very much and will show his or her love any way he or she can, but not in every way you need. You have not done anything wrong, nor has the person you reached out to. Accept that there are some kinds of love only you can provide for yourself. It is ultimately your responsibility to fill this need. Practice showing yourself kindness and compassion.

447. Try not to pass on an opportunity just because it is not ideal. You may have an idea in your mind about what your path to your ideal future looks like. Be open to small changes and alternative ways to achieve what you want. If you wait around for what you think is the perfect opportunity, you might miss out on more realistic ways to progress in the direction you want to go.

448. Contemplate changing your attitude about what fair looks like. You might be attempting to fight to receive the same resources and opportunities as others, but you may be reaching out for the wrong type of support. It might not be what you need. Fair is getting what you need, not necessarily getting the same as others. Since you are unique, what you need is probably also unique.

449. There is little need to attract a large audience. You may wish to reach out for support, which is fine, but try to draw a line. Make sure you do not share so much that you violate healthy boundaries. Not every little thing needs to be shared with a wide audience online via a blog or video. Part of the healing process probably involves practicing self-validation, which is difficult if you share too much information with others. Start to keep a private journal to begin the work of validating parts of your life. Sharing is good, but you can keep it healthy.

450. You deserve to live your life well. You are of equal worth on some basic level with all other people on the planet. You have an equal right to live and to pursue a healthy life that you enjoy. Refrain from listening to any viewpoint, even if it is your own, telling you otherwise.

451. Most likely you are not better off alone. You may find being around people energy draining, but continue to seek out company. Isolation may increase the severity of clinical depression symptoms.

You may feel like you are pushing people away, but your perception might be an exaggeration. It is okay if a social situation does not go well. Keep attempting to reestablish or create new healthy relationships with others.

452. It is okay if you do not fit in. You are going through a very unique experience. You are undergoing a lot of change, which may leave you feeling like you do not belong in many of the places that before made you feel safe. Such an experience is not uncommon. Clinical depression is a severe medical condition that possibly will impact many aspects of your life, including where you feel most comfortable.

453. Something does not have to have a purpose in order to matter. You may experience many things that matter a great deal, but do not really serve any purpose for you. That is okay. At times there is no logical reason why something is happening, but it still is very real. It is fine to admit it all matters. Your life matters, the events of today matter, and even your problems matter.

454. It is okay if you feel fragmented. Living with a severe medical condition or dealing with major life problems may cause you to feel incomplete or divided. Practice actions that are aligned with your beliefs and priorities. As you continue to work towards creating a healthier future, you likely will find yourself feeling more whole.

455. Create a personalized emergency safety plan. When living with a severe medical condition, it probably is a really good idea to put in place some kind of plan to fall back on if your symptoms become extremely severe. What this plan would entail exactly would be up to you to decide. It might include a recipe for your favorite cookies, a list of your favorite parks to visit, suggestions of movies to watch, or ideas on how to distract yourself with busyness. You might get really creative and actually make a safety box filled with stuff to aid and comfort you. How you go about it is your decision, but the options are almost endless.

456. Suicidal thinking is not a sign of weakness. Rather, it is a sign that you are simply not well right now. You have done nothing wrong. Sometimes, despite your best attempts, these thoughts may happen. It is okay to talk about this symptom if you are experiencing it. It is always fine to ask for help and assistance.

457. Consider singing a song. Occasionally you may find that singing along to your favorite tune or inventing your own music brings you some peace. You may find it very freeing to express yourself in this manner. It doesn't have to be fancy or sung with company. You can sing along with the radio while driving or hum your favorite childhood songs in the shower. It is just another way to incorporate music in a manner that you might find helpful.

458. It is ultimately your responsibility to seek out treatment. Reliance on others to pull you out of your home and drag you off to visit with some kind of medical professional is not a realistic way to approach your situation. Most likely, many of the symptoms of clinical depression cannot be observed, but are often only felt by the individual experiencing them. If you feel that you might be experiencing symptoms of a severe medical condition, ask for help getting to a doctor, ask for assistance in making an appointment, or even request company during the travel there, but remember it is your responsibility to request help.

459. Consider making a positive set of images and words. You can make a set of flashcards with your favorite quotes and sayings. You could also make a notebook filled with pictures or create a space online with your favorite digital photography. Having a collection of uplifting thoughts and imagines may reduce stress and increase your happiness level.

460. Try to read every day. Read articles or books. Read magazines or online blogs. Read about topics you find interesting in the format that appeals to you most. Reading is a habit that you can continue to practice regardless of your state of mental health. Do not worry about how much you are reading. It is okay if you can only read for a few minutes at a time. Just try your best to keep reading and learning each day.

461. Try to not complain for an hour or even a whole day. By choosing to go complaint free, you are regaining some control over how you respond to negative thoughts. You are making a short term commitment to a more positive way of responding to some of the most destructive thoughts in your mind. It may take several attempts before you can let go of the complaints. You are not a failure if you fail to reach your goal on the first try, so be kind to yourself.

462. Create a list of your positive qualities. The first time you make this list, it may not have as many items as you might like. That is okay. Keep this list some place safe where you can easily get to it again. When you are having a rough time, it might help to reread it and remind yourself about all of your positive virtues and talents. You can also add to it as you think of more traits you value in yourself.

463. Sometimes all you need is faith in yourself. There are times when you might not have every single resource that you want in your possession before you see an opportunity you wish to take advantage of. You can go ahead and try to benefit from the chance you have discovered. Just by placing a bit of faith in your ability to capitalize on a good situation, you may find that you can do a lot more than you originally realized.

464. Envision sending obsessions away from your mind. You might try creating an image that you can go to when you feel that you may be obsessing. You can put your obsessions in a big box, lock it, and throw away the key. You could picture closing a door to shut the obsession out. You may even imagine mailing it to a location far away. Practice different visions until one suits you.

465. Others do not have to cooperate. You may have a fantastic plan. You may have thought about it forwards and backwards. You may know that it has no flaws at all and yet you might still encounter someone who refuses to cooperate. It happens. Everyone, including you, has the right to not go along with an idea or plan. Try not to waste your time hoping for people to change, just make small changes to your plan or change your expectations.

466. Make a list of things you have done well. One way to give yourself recognition is to write down all your achievements at the end of each day. You might also try just saying them aloud or otherwise acknowledging all of the things you have accomplished. You get to decide what is noteworthy, so validate as many things as you wish.

467. Before doing something new, make a plan. Consider your expectations before trying something different. Spend a few minutes contemplating what the outcome might be if the new thing does not meet your expectations. Give yourself permission to try something new and be okay if it is not fun or otherwise delightful. Give yourself credit for trying and think of new things you might like to do. With practice, trying new stuff will get easier.

468. Stick to specifics when you ask for things you want. Even if you speak up and request something, without giving details, it might still be hard to receive what you want. Making a general statement about how you would like to go out more, spend more time alone, or get more attention probably will not result in getting what you actually want. Try stating details like on what days you wish to go out and where you want to visit. Try explaining how you define being alone as just being in a room by yourself or maybe you really do want the house to free of company. Consider stating that you want eye contact from a family member when you speak or perhaps the kind of attention you seek is just the opportunity to spend more time with others. Being direct most likely will result in more success.

469. Consider reaching out to people who have had clinical depression and recovered. You may find some comfort in talking to other individuals who have survived depression. You may learn some helpful tips or coping strategies. It might provide you with opportunities to ask pressing questions or gain some wisdom about living with the condition.

470. Choose to be aware of nonverbal communication. When you are having a conversation, keep in mind how your tone of voice, body language, and facial expressions might alter the meaning of the words you are speaking. Some of these aspects of communication may have seemed to come naturally to you before, but now might take more effort. It is okay if you accidently communicate more than you mean to when speaking with others. Just be more mindful of nonverbal behavior and continue practicing your best.

471. Collect information about risks. You can prepare yourself before taking a possible risk. It is important to not obsess about preparedness. Taking the time to understand different possible outcomes might reduce your stress and you will most certainly have realistic expectations regarding how you will fare from the experience.

472. Express yourself in a safe and healthy manner. You can choose from a large number of positive activities to express your unique perspective. Being creative is a popular way to explore your viewpoint, but there are other methods too. Building and making anything might greatly relax you and provide a sense of accomplishment. Expressing yourself does not have to be original, like a piece of art. It just simply needs to be something that you find a positive experience.

473. Practice identifying the skills you need for your goals. Deciding what goals you wish to work on is only part of the journey to achievement. Take time to list all the skills you think you might need to reach your goal and include the skills you already possess. Knowing what to practice in order to move forward towards the future you are creating for yourself is most certainly beneficial for you.

474. You can take a short break from your problems. There is no need to constantly think about what ails you. It is okay if you take a few minutes to think about anything else, to distract yourself from your troubles. Giving yourself a brief break might help you gain some clarity about the situation.

475. You might not reach your dreams and that is okay. Actually finishing your biggest, wildest dream to its absolute end is not really what the road to recovery from a major medical condition looks like. In actuality, you most certainly will not have to wait that long for recovery. What changes you, grows you, and makes you stronger is simply the process of working towards a massive achievement. If you achieve your biggest dream, then that undoubtedly will make you feel wonderful. However, making it to that great big finish line is not a requirement for enjoyment or for success. It is all the little stuff that drives you there that will make you happier, more empowered, and will in time completely heal you.

476. How you react to the events of your life is extremely important. You cannot control all aspects of yourself or all the things that will happen to you. What most often is within your control is how you choose to respond. You are capable of choosing to respond in a healthy manner. You have the strength to select behavior that supports you and does not bring you further down. This is always your choice.

477. List the benefits you will experience once you reach your goal. It might be helpful to actually write down the benefits you expect to receive next to your goals. You may want to incorporate these benefits into your decision to select one goal over another.

Defining the outcomes you anticipate, even for small daily goals, may possibly motivate you and reduce anxiety.

478. You do not need to prove someone wrong in order to be happy, successful, or healthy. Your self-worth and overall state of mind is not contingent on a series of events that demonstrate or show someone how valuable you are. There is no life requirement that states you must prove your boss, parent, or friend wrong before moving forward in your life. You can move forward and onwards whenever you wish. You can work towards being happy, successful, and healthy without being spiteful.

479. Take the time to ask if your goals are realistically attainable. You might get excited about discovering a goal that you want to work towards and forget to take a hard look at how long it might take to achieve it. You also may need to examine your abilities and strengths. Responsible goal planning requires more from you than just a desire to achieve. It also requires your commitment to be honest about your intent.

480. Make appointments with your problems. Another strategy that might help relieve a lot of anxiety is to schedule time to sit down and think about a problem. You can reserve a window of time to analyze the problem and think of possible solutions. You might spend the time brainstorming ways to find or create solutions. For full effectiveness, resist the urge to think about your problem in between appointments and define the problem in as specific of terms as you are capable.

481. Your sense of humor might change and that is okay. What was once funny to you might just seem boring or a waste of time. It is fine. As you grow and change, the things that amuse you most certainly will change too. Explore new types of comedy and be patient. It may be a while before you rediscover your sense of humor.

482. Choose to be a selective worrier. There may be many things that you wish to worry about, but there is no need. Be picky about what you spend your time thinking about. Try to focus on only one worry at a time, if any at all. You have the power to prioritize what you are concerned about.

483. Needing several support systems is not a sign you are extra needy. As a human, you are unique and at times complex. That is just the reality of the human experience. It is also the case that your needs are not going to be met via one helpful person, one activity, or one type of support. Instead, ponder the benefits of different types of support systems. Reach out to family and friends, but also look into joining a therapeutic support group. Look towards your spiritual beliefs, but do not be too hard on yourself if you look at new philosophies for guidance. Practice your hobbies, but do not worry if you want to try something new. You are a unique person so it makes sense that you need a unique network of stuff to aid you in your recovery.

484. Do an everyday activity differently. You are able to positively impact your everyday environment. Change how you fold your clothes. Make something new for breakfast, or you could experiment with different ways of cleaning the dishes. You might discover a method that works better for you that you then can adopt into your daily routine.

485. Write your own definition of success. Avoid allowing expectations invented by other people dictate what your success should look and feel like. You have the power and the right to decide when you are successful. Your achievements are met when you say they have been. You are successful when you believe to be so. Just keep in mind that while living with a severe medical condition, your ability to determine how exactly you feel might be impacted. For this reason, be cautious, but remember that this does not mean you no longer have the ability to decide what is meaningful to you.

486. Write down positive thoughts. Create a safe place to record your positive thoughts about anything and everything. Seriously contemplate making a notebook filled with these thoughts. Decorate the pages they fill. At first, you may only have a few thoughts to write down and that is okay. In time, it will grow. Keep this in a safe place and reread it often.

487. Take action to protect what you find meaningful. Identify what you value and then make decisions consistently to guard your values. Be open to allowing some flexibility when you experience situations that test your values and also be open to modifying them. This process of living your life with your values as a guide can help you grow and heal.

488. Be kind to all aspects of yourself. A mental illness impacts more than just your mental self. It also impacts your spiritual, physical, and emotional self. For any treatment plan to be fully effective, it most certainly will include ways to aid all parts of you that are suffering. To further complicate matters, you may experience recovery in one area of yourself, but other areas are still in a negative state. It is okay. The road to recovery is complex.

489. It is okay to be wrong. You may spend a lot of time fighting to be correct and right about what is happening in your life. However, insisting on being right is also insisting on being perfect, which is not a very healthy mindset. It often is better to accept when you are wrong because you can more easily forgive and be open to changing what you need to.

490. Choose to recognize what is already working effectively and keep doing it. Take the time to identify which aspects are already effective. You may discover a problem that at first seems massive is actually not quite as bad once you list all of the things that are already going in your favor. You may possibly find a pattern. You could discover things that you do which are not adding to your suffering or pain in any way. Continue to do what is already working well.

491. Conflict and frustration are normal parts of relationships. Disagreements are common and typical. You are not a bad person just because you encounter conflict in one of your relationships. The important aspect to focus on is how you behave and react to the conflict. No matter how you feel about a person or situation, you can still treat all involved, including yourself, with respect.

492. Refrain from trying to place blame. For many things in life, there just is simply no one at fault. If you obsess over trying to find someone or something to blame, you miss out on simply living your life to the fullest extent possible. There is a huge difference between accepting blame and taking responsibility. Focus more on owning your responsibility. You can use it to empower yourself by taking control and making changes to better suit your needs.

493. Identify your needs versus your wants. Spend time and effort differentiating between what you need to be healthy and what you simply just want. Be honest and real about your needs. You do need things that help your mental, social, and emotional health just as badly as things for your physical health. Practice asking for things that you need and be honest about how much you really need them. Try asking for things that you want too, but be truthful about how they are simply things you want. You may have times when you can only obtain what you need, so do not waste resources gathering stuff you want at the cost of things you need.

494. Bad things do not have to ruin the good stuff. What you know and believe to be good can still be good. A single bad event, idea, or object does not necessarily rob your life of any of its goodness. If one oozes into another then that is most likely a result of your actions. Choose to isolate the bad and let it go. Allow goodness to stay with you for as long as you wish it to.

495. Focus on what you can control right now. There will always be things you can control and things that you cannot. Apply your energy to things that are within your control that you wish to change. Alter them so they are healthier for you. It will take some practice, but in time, you can build a much more positive life for yourself.

496. Harming others for your benefit or amusement is never appropriate. There are many ways to achieve your goals. Choose a path that does not involve hurting anyone. This also includes you. It is possible with practice to live a healthier life. There is no need to resort to being anything less than a kind, compassionate person when working on creating a better future.

497. Reexamine how you think stress benefits you. Having a lot of commitments, worries, or an overwhelming schedule does not make you more important or a harder worker. It just makes you more stressed. Avoid the temptation to put overwhelming pressure on yourself. Living with clinical depression is a huge strain on your overall health. Do your best to be your finest friend and ease up on stress inducing expectations.

498. You are strong. The truth is that clinical depression is a strenuous condition. After living with it for one day, you have become one of the strongest people on the planet. You survived and demonstrated resilience. You are capable of continuing on your quest to a better, healthier life. You deserve to continue, so take your strength and hold on. Hold on to this moment, let it become another hour and another day. Welcome tomorrow with optimism. Live your life, now stronger and wiser for no other reason than because deep down, there is at least a small part of you that really wants to.

499. You might have to invent or create what you need and that is okay. The world has not failed you nor have you failed yourself. It just may be the case that you figured out what you need in order to achieve a healthier life and no one else has made it yet. Go ahead and get started designing and contriving. Make the tools and resources you need. You deserve to pursue your goals.

500. You are not alone. Many currently are living with a form of clinical depression. Many more have family or friends battling with this severe medical condition. Sadly, some have lost their lives to the mental illness, but there are many who have survived it. It is possible to rise from this situation. You have the ability and strength. You might feel alone right now, and that is okay. Just know that life has not abandoned you, the future has not disowned you, and today is just a temporary thing that will pass through you. You will persevere.

www.ingramcontent.com/pod-product-compliance
Lightning Source LLC
Chambersburg PA
CBHW071858020426
42331CB00010B/2577